REUTERS CENTURY OF GREAT BRITISH SPORT

MIKE NEWLIN
WITH
TIMOTHY COLLINGS

CollinsWillow
An Imprint of HarperCollins*Publishers*

First published in 1999 by CollinsWillow
an imprint of HarperCollins*Publishers*
London

1 3 5 7 9 8 6 4 2

A CIP catalogue record for this book is available from the British Library

The HarperCollins website address is:
www.**fire**and**water**.co.uk

ISBN 0 00 218950 X

Editor: Chris Stone
Designer: GDAdesign

Colour reproduction by Colourscan Singapore
Printed and bound in Italy by Rotolito Lombarda

CONTENTS

FOREWORD

Steve Parry joined Reuters Sports Desk in 1966. He has been Sports Editor since 1982. He has covered 15 Summer and Winter Olympics and a dozen World Cups and Commonwealth Games.

There were few hints of the shape of things to come in the world of sport when I joined Reuters in 1966. The Olympics, like Reuters, were non-profit-making and most sports were still amateur, or more accurately 'shamateur' since illegal payments were rife. England had not yet won the World Cup, Israeli athletes had not yet been murdered at the Munich Olympics, Hillsborough and Heysel were only the stuff of nightmares and doping was something you did to model aeroplanes.

But the past 20 years have seen an explosion of top-class events based on an alliance of sport, sponsorship and television, so that the global sports industry now has an estimated annual turnover of £250 billion. Reuters sports coverage, once aimed solely at newspapers and broadcasters, now flows into all corners of an ever-expanding market with text, pictures, graphics and television offered to a multitude of Internet sites, databases and financial services as well as the traditional print and broadcast media.

Equally significant have been the developments in information systems and communications which have given unprecedented mobility to the modern reporter armed with laptop computer and mobile phone. But readers have become more sophisticated too, so that yesterday's reporting standards do not always hold good for today.

Thirty years ago the typical wire service sports report was often worthy but dull. But the immediacy of television has forced the written media to dig deeper for the story behind the story. Gone too are the days when the sports reporter simply covered sport.

The Munich massacre and the Olympic boycotts of the 1970s and 1980s obliged sports specialists to acquire some understanding of international politics, while the more recent IOC scandal has taken them into the murky realms of bribery and corruption. A grasp of the financial markets has also become a must as soccer clubs across Europe queue up to launch stock flotations. It's all a far cry from what now seems to have been an age of innocence, but probably never was.

My own involvement with sport stretches back half a century to the 1948 London Olympics when I lived about a javelin's throw from Wembley Stadium. During the 1948 Olympics my parents invited a member of the Mexican boxing team to stay with us during the Games and 20 years later I found myself in Mexico City covering boxing at my first Olympics for Reuters.

Having been asked to introduce this celebration of 100 years of British sport, I decided to dip into *The Power of News*, the history of Reuters by Donald Read, to find the first recorded sports item on the Reuters wire. This turned out to be a story relating to the last bare knuckle fight in England, the 1860 scrap between Englishman Tom Sayers and American John Heenan in which they fought for 37 rounds before the referee fled to avoid being beaten up by ringside rowdies. The pair battled on for five more rounds before a draw was declared.

Public interest in sport had become intense throughout the British Empire by 1900 and boxing, cricket, soccer, rugby and horse racing results and reports were sent regularly to colonial subscribers in Africa, Asia and Australasia. A couple of decades later Reuters reported on the first Wembley FA Cup final in 1923 when a crowd estimated at between 200,000 and 250,000 spilled on to the pitch before order was famously restored by a policeman on a white horse. Since then, the match has always been known as the 'White Horse' final.

By this time other annual British sporting delights such as Wimbledon tennis, the Henley rowing regatta and the Oxford-Cambridge University boat race had been added to the file. The 1923 boat race produced an early example of the sort of error that haunts sub-editors the world over when Oxford's winning distance was given as three-quarters of a mile instead of three-quarters of a length.

Until the advent of laptop communications, stories were often dictated to a copy-taker with the inevitable risk of telephonic mis-hearings which could elude a weary and frazzled sub, sometimes with bizarre results. My two favourites, both

genuine Reuters offerings, concerned the men's Olympic heavyweight judo champion who was described as 'a 26-year-old nightclub dancer' (instead of bouncer) and a mysterious phrase from the 1978 World Cup which described someone as 'a bloody slow two-baller.' It turned out to be a reference to Spain's Hungarian-born coach, Ladislao Kubala. Reuters had four copy-takers on this assignment, none of whom had English as a first language!

The risk of error was just as great in the days of cabled copy when Reuters devised various codes to compress the length of telegraphic messages and save money. For example, a Test cricket score might be cabled to London as a single word such as GUUKKAFY. A sub-editor would pore over his code book and deduce that rain had stopped play (GU), the score was 76 (UK) for two (KA) and that lunch (FY) was being taken.

But the perils of getting it hopelessly wrong were spectacularly illustrated on 28 June 1914 with the assassination of Archduke Franz Ferdinand at Sarajevo, which triggered the outbreak of the First World War. The first news of the assassination was given in a terse phone call to London from Reuters' Paris office which advised in French: 'Sarajevo Ferdinand Assassinated.' Unfortunately the sub-editor who took the call was awaiting the result of the Grand Prix de Paris horse race. The hapless individual assumed this was the message he had received and prepared a report on the lines of: The result of the Grand Prix de Paris this afternoon was:
1. SARAJEVO.
2. FERDINAND.
3. ASSASSINATED.
Happily, a more senior editor realised the true significance of the Paris message and intervened before the ludicrous 'race result' could be issued.

Assassinations apart, the biggest challenge to any sportswriter is the Olympics, although Reuters seem to have got off to an inauspicious start at the first modern Games in Athens in 1896 when results and descriptive appeared only sporadically, apparently at the whim of a local freelance.

But by 1936 German propaganda chief Josef Goebbels recognised the importance of Reuters in covering the Berlin Olympics and allocated a privileged viewing box to sports editor Vernon Morgan, one of Reuters' colourful characters. He ran in the steeplechase at the 1928 Amsterdam Olympics, held the South African allcomers' mile record for over 20 years and played one match for Manchester United in 1925.

More than half a century later he was a consultant on the film script for *Chariots of Fire*. Morgan had the manner of a genial 19th century squire and was fondly known as 'the Baron' to a generation of sports reporters around the world.

He was sports editor from 1933 to 1968, having joined Reuters in 1931 – a year after the exotic Bernard Rickatson-Hatt became New York correspondent with a taste for sports reporting. In *The Power of News*, Read notes that Hatt, a future editor-in-chief, had the military bearing of a former Coldstream Guards officer, complete with monocle, bowler hat and rolled umbrella – but there were oddities. 'Hatt's complexion was abnormally pink and white, and he was suspected of wearing a corset. He often came to the office bearing a small poodle.' Exotic or not, Hatt was clearly forceful enough to make an impact on the tough American boxing scene of the 1930s. According to one anecdote, a fight at Madison Square Garden was once delayed to await his late arrival at the ringside.

The value placed on Reuters' sports coverage by subscribers was apparent even in wartime when in 1941, with Malta under siege, the owner of *The Times* of Malta cabled London requesting a 'full list of Derby runners as soon as possible.' This has been borne out in more recent years when worldwide use of Reuters coverage from the Olympics or World Cup has sometimes exceeded the total of non-sporting general news stories. A senior Reuters editor once complained that it made no sense to spend money on sports coverage because it was all so trivial. 'Yes,' I explained. 'That's why it's so popular.'

STEVE PARRY
Sports Editor Reuters
London

1900-1909

THE EARLY HEROES

1

NOTHING SUMS UP THE compelling nature of British sport better than the way Manchester United came back to win the 1999 European Cup final. Two goals in added time, after the clock had passed the 90 minutes mark, not only turned the match on its head, they also left the spectators, not to mention the players, dumbfounded. It was live and unscripted drama, pure sporting exhilaration, and it released the kind of joy that is unique to such gallant events.

It was a triumph for the bulldog spirit against one of its oldest adversaries – drilled Teutonic technique – in a festival of colour and sound. It brought back memories of the 1966 World Cup final, when extra-time was needed before England overcame West Germany, and the 1968 European final when the same United, inspired like England by Bobby Charlton, also needed another half an hour in which to defeat Eusebio's Benfica. Heroic deeds all, just like the feats of WG Grace, CB Fry, Dixie Dean, Fred Perry, Len Hutton, Tommy Lawton, Frank Swift, Fred Trueman, Matt Busby, Stirling Moss, Lester Piggott, Jim Clark, Jackie Stewart, Willie John McBride, Mary Peters, Ian Botham, Sebastian Coe and the rest of those men and women whose actions made sporting headlines and punctuated the everyday lives of us all.

In essence, then, not much has changed in the course of the 20th century. Or has it? Commercialism, instant global media coverage, sponsorship, marketing and almost-fantastic levels of fitness and commitment to competition have raised the standards and the spectacle in every way. But the basic lure of the live event remains. For every Manchester United fan who travelled to Barcelona for that final on May 26, it was being there that mattered on a night that will never be forgotten. Thirty-one years after winning it for the only previous time, their team touched the heights in such compelling style that, as a story of guts and courage, it had overwhelming human power. And that, forever, remains the quality that lies at the heart of British sport.

Artistry is always appreciated, organisation is respected and the energy of youth enjoyed. But nothing touches the depths of the ordinary man like an unexpected recovery from the edge of defeat. And that is why British sport, laced with its own disasters and tragedies, intrigues and adventures, has become such an integral part of our culture and its heroes are such icons

BILL 'FATTY' FOULKE AND THE BALL-BOYS

When Gus Mears took Chelsea to Stamford Bridge and into the Football League, he gave responsibility for player recruitment to his manager, the former Rangers and Scotland player John Robertson. Immediately, he set to work north of the border and he brought many men to London. His most famous acquisition, however, came not from Scotland, but from Sheffield United. He was Bill 'Fatty' Foulke, (back row centre) who weighed more than 22 stone and had an enormous waistline as well as surprising agility. To emphasise this, it was said, Chelsea positioned two boys behind his goal as a distraction. Ball-boys were thus invented.

Above: The Doherty brothers, Reggie and Laurie, won eight consecutive Wimbledon doubles titles between 1897-1905.

in our modern heritage. From the start, it has been that way. CB Fry was not just a sportsman. He was an example. He was an embodiment of the sporting spirit of his time as much as David Beckham has been of his.

Fry, of course, is also the man whose name is synonymous with what were once called Corinthian values, or sportsmanship, and the emergence of sport as a mass spectator interest at the turn of the 20th century. A brilliant cricketer and footballer, he played in the FA Cup as a schoolboy and, in 1893, set a long jump world record when he was 21. He gained Oxford blues for athletics, cricket and football, and played for Southampton, for whom he appeared in the 1902 FA Cup final, and England in the latter. As a cricketer, he made 94 first-class centuries, including a record six in succession, in 1901, for Sussex. He almost added a rugby blue to his collection, but was injured. Regarded as a renaissance man, he captained England and played in 26 Test matches, setting a standard in all-round excellence that has rarely been equalled. For that, he has become the touchstone of British sport.

Fry stood high already, then, as the sporting century unfolded with the Olympic Games of 1900 in Paris, the birthplace of Pierre de Coubertin. It was an ambitious shambles, as an event, and featured the oddity of live pigeon shooting, for the only time. In this contest, Crittenden Robinson of Britain tied third after killing 19 birds, thus taking a bronze medal. In that first year of this century, 1900, the Prince

of Wales' horse Ambush II prompted wild hat-throwing and cheers by winning the Grand National at Liverpool, AE Stoddart scored 221 against Somerset when he returned to cricket after an absence of 18 months, in a benefit game for Middlesex bowler JT Hearne, and Reggie Doherty – the Wimbledon-born tennis-player – won the men's singles at the Wimbledon championships for the fourth successive year. He and his brother Laurie also won the Olympic doubles gold in Paris and the Wimbledon doubles, achievements which were to lead to the south-east gates being named after them. Such successes seem almost incredible now, viewed from the other end of the century, when English cricket and tennis is less than a tour-de-force.

Football, then as now, held a firm grip on

ALF COMMON AND THE FIRST £1,000 TRANSFER

It was, said the *Athletic News*, quite extraordinary. 'Every club has its price,' the news chronicle revealed. 'But what a price.' The shock was caused by Middlesbrough's decision to pay £1,000 for the England centre-forward Alf Common. They signed him from near-neighbours Sunderland. 'As a matter of commerce,' the paper continued, '10 young recruits at £100 apiece might have paid better and as a matter of sport the Second Division would be more honourable than retention of place by purchase.' Who, in the football world of the late 1990s, would be so scandalised by any club attempting to buy itself out of trouble? Common's goals did succeed in keeping Middlesbrough up, his humour and ruddy health allowing him to steer away from trouble. His record-breaking move in February, 1905, however, never left him alone.

the public imagination. In 1901, while former players began the tradition of complaining at the rampant commercialisation – then in the form of transfer fees and wages – which was perceived to be ruining their game, Tottenham Hotspur became the first non-league team to win the FA Cup. As a Southern League side, they beat Sheffield United 3-1 in a replay at Bolton, following a 2-2 draw at Crystal Palace watched by 114,815. The winning treble strike came from Sandy Brown (who scored in every round) but the lasting significance of this final, greater even than the record size of the crowd, was provided by Tottenham officials at their post-match celebration dinner. There, they attached ribbons to the cup in their colours and started a tradition which has never died.

The following season, 1902, football experienced its first great tragedy of the century when, on April 5, a grandstand collapsed at Ibrox Park, Glasgow. Twenty-five people died and more than 500 were injured after a section of terracing fell in during the opening minutes of Scotland's match against England. Surprisingly, the game continued, to prevent panic, and many in the 70,000 crowd knew nothing of the deaths until they read of them in the evening papers. The result was 1-1, but the match was declared unofficial and replayed in Birmingham a month later when all the receipts went to the disaster fund.

The same year saw an Englishman, Selwyn Edge, win the Gordon Bennett Cup, inaugurated by an American newspaper tycoon living in Paris, for proving fastest over the 350-mile stage to Innsbruck, run within the structure of the Paris-Vienna motor car race. Edge's win, in a Napier, ended the dominance of French drivers and cars in the event.

Elsewhere, Alexander 'Sandy' Herd of Huddersfield won the Open golf championship at Hoylake, using a 'new' Haskell golf ball, and

Left: The 1901 FA Cup final at Crystal Palace between Tottenham Hotspur and Sheffield United.
Below: The collapsed terracing at Ibrox Park which claimed the lives of 25 supporters in 1902.

CB Fry played on the losing side for Southampton in their replayed FA Cup final defeat by Sheffield United, two matches which sandwiched an appearance by Fry as opening batsman for London County against Surrey. He hit 82 and 49 not out, just two days after the first final.

In 1903, as sporting activity gained momentum, Laurie Doherty shone again at Wimbledon, Wales beat England by three goals and two tries to one goal in front of a rejoicing 30,000 crowd at Swansea and Harry Vardon won the Open golf championship at Prestwick, his fourth triumph. If that was not enough, RE 'Tip' Foster made his cricket debut for England against Australia in Sydney and scored a record 287. England won the Test by five wickets and went on to take the Ashes home by three wins to two, the following March.

At Wimbledon, in 1904, the Dohertys maintained their doubles dominance (they won eight doubles titles in all) while, at Troon, another famous all-rounder, Lottie Dod of Moreton, won the Ladies' Open golf championship, adding it to her various tennis titles. Her successes proved the popularity of sport to both sexes at a time when football was organising itself in Paris, on May 21, into an international federation with the formation of FIFA. England joined the original seven in 1905, a year which also saw the creation of the modern Chelsea at Stamford Bridge, thanks to Gus Mears and his brother taking over the London Athletic Club site.

These, of course, were the years of sporting growth during which the seeds of the

Below: Italy's Dorando Pietri is helped over the line in the 1908 Olympic marathon.
Right: WG Grace. His phenomenal batting averages are part of cricketing legend.

organisations – which were to rule the century – were sown and great players were born or began their careers. Frank Woolley, in 1906, began his record-breaking cricket career with Kent, while Athens hosted the 'intermediate' Olympic Games and France, in their first official rugby union international, beat England 35-8 at the Parc des Princes. Not a bad start. Liverpudlians celebrated, too, after Liverpool won the Football League title and Everton the FA Cup.

Evidence that English rugby was not all-powerful was offered again in 1907 at Swansea when the national team was humbled 22-0 by a Wales side which fielded a pack of seven against England's eight and, therefore, an extra back. Such trickery paid off to the passionate delight of about 17,500 spectators who braved incessant drizzle. Welsh rugby players were often said to be the red dragons of their country personified in mud and this was one of those days. But the same year saw other bold happenings: the opening of Brooklands, the first purpose-built motor racing circuit in the world, in Surrey; Middlesbrough forward Steve Bloomer's final appearance for England leaving him with a record of 28 goals in 23 matches; and Glasgow Celtic winning the 'double' in Scotland, the first club to do so.

In 1908, the Olympic Games came to London. One of the outstanding episodes of the event was provided by the Italian runner

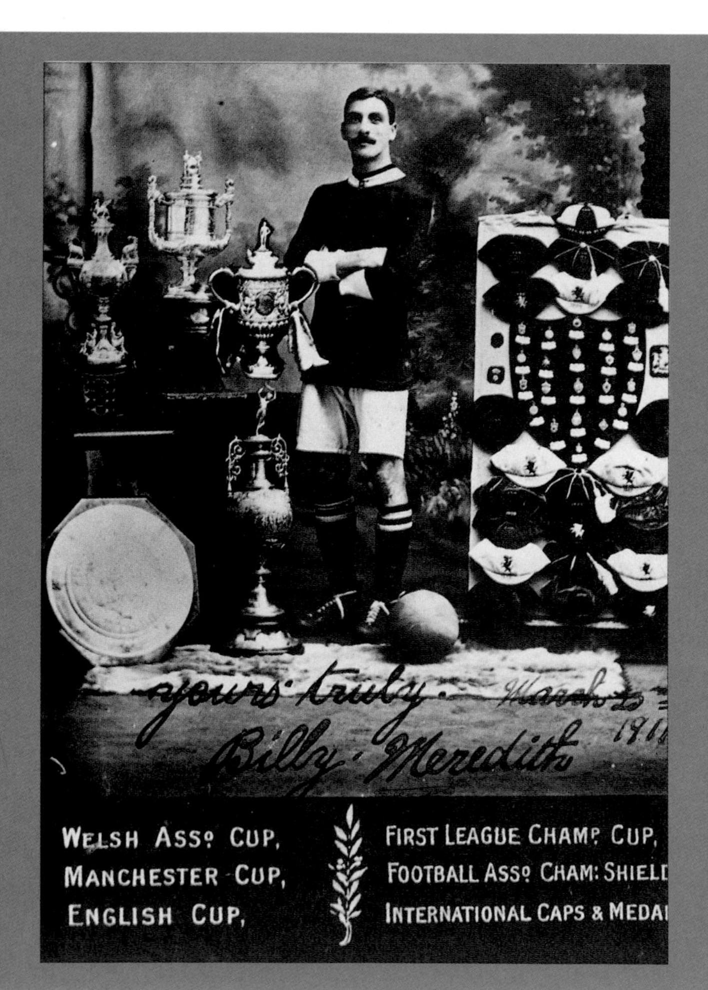

BILLY MEREDITH AND THE MAXIMUM WAGE STRUGGLE

It may be unbelievable now, but in 1907 a Manchester United star player, who shone on the pitch during his team's championship-winning season, helped lead the revolt against the maximum wage of £4 per week. Billy Meredith, a mainstay of the United side in the winter of 1907-1908, chaired the inaugural meeting of the Players' Union at the Imperial Hotel, Manchester, on December 2. More than 500 players attended. Within a month, it had embraced southern and northern players in the same organisation. One of their chief objectives was to remove the maximum wage and gain freedom of contract. It took them a lot longer than they thought it would and it was not until the 1960s and the 1990s that such ambitions were to be realised.

Meredith, a brilliant right-winger with Northwich Victoria, Manchester City (twice), Manchester United and Wales, won his first cap in 1895 and his last in 1920, at the age of 45 years and 229 days, when Wales beat England for the first time. He created the record of being the oldest player ever to win international honours. He won an FA Cup winner's medal with both City and United and won League Championships with United twice. Known as the 'prince of wingers', he had a laconic style and played with a toothpick in his mouth.

WG GRACE AND THE CREATION OF ENGLISH CRICKET

Dr William Gilbert Grace was born in Downend, Bristol, on July 18, 1848 and died in Mottingham, Kent, on October 23, 1915. In between those dates, in arguably cricket's most famous passage of time, he took a game that was seen as a glorious rural pastime and turned it into a national pursuit of sporting significance. Dubbed 'the champion', WG bestrode those years as exactly that.

His beard, his full figure, his image as a portly middle-aged man who was still playing Test cricket at 50, became synonymous with the sound of leather on willow, white flannels and summer birdsong. He made his last first-class appearance at the age of 60 in 1908, but his career was littered with such statistical landmarks and records. In 1871, he was the first player to exceed 2000 runs in a season and made a record 10 centuries. He made the first triple-century in first-class cricket for the MCC against Kent in 1876, scoring 344. A few days later, he hit 316 for Gloucestershire against Yorkshire.

In 1875, just to prove he was once a high-quality all-rounder, he took 191 wickets at an average of 12.94, rolling round-arm. He did the double of 1000 runs and 100 wickets eight times, played for Gloucestershire for 31 years (from 1868 to 1899) and, in 1866, during an England v Surrey clash at the Oval, performed the extraordinary feat of scoring 224 and, on a day when he was absent from the cricket, ran at Crystal Palace, in the National Olympic Association meeting, where he won the 440 yards hurdles.

In 1903, he was elected president of the English Bowling Association. He played in 22 Test matches from 1880 to 1899, scoring 1098 runs at an average of 32.29 and played first-class cricket from 1865 to 1908, scoring 54,896 runs at an average of 39.55. Some career, some cricketer.

Above: JH Taylor (centre) wins the 1909 Open championship at Deal.

SYDNEY BARNES, GREATEST BOWLER OF ALL TIME?

Born at Smethwick in Staffordshire, in 1873, Sydney Barnes has been called the greatest bowler of all by many critics. He had a perfect action and could swing or spin, but he was a lofty maverick who played only 10 England Test matches and limited cricket for Warwickshire and Lancashire. But his Test record is extraordinary. In South Africa, in 1913-1914, in four matches, he took 49 wickets at an average of 10.93. This included a match analysis of 17-159 (8-56 and 9-103), a record that stood until beaten by Jim Laker in 1956. He took 189 Test wickets in all and 6229 in his first-class career at an average of 8.33, playing many of his matches for Staffordshire in the Minor Counties Championship.

Dorando Pietri who led the marathon – run from Windsor Castle to the specially-built stadium in London – until he fell again and again on his last lap before, with the aid of officials, struggled to breast the tape. He was disqualified for receiving assistance and the American Johnny Hayes was declared the winner. But the little man from Italy had captured the hearts of all 60,000 spectators and, when Queen Alexandra presented the prizes, she called afterwards for Pietri and gave him a personal gift of a gold cup to mark his efforts. His was an Olympian effort.

In the same year, one of cricket's greatest names, if not the greatest of all, retired. WG Grace – his huge frame, long and full beard, big personality and ability to score runs and take wickets with equal aplomb – withdrew from the first-class game. He had scored 54,896 runs, including 126 centuries, and taken 2,876 wickets. In July, 1908, he celebrated his 60th birthday. A remarkable man. Notable, by comparison, was Manchester United's feat that same Spring in winning the Football League Championship by nine points.

The next year, 1909, was to be overshadowed by another black football day in Scotland, this time a whisky-fuelled riot at Hampden Park in Glasgow following the replayed Scottish Cup final between Rangers and Celtic. Both matches ended in draws, 2-2 and 1-1, but the second was followed by mayhem as spectators ran amok, tore down the goals, cut up the pitch and set fire to the pay-boxes and the stands, using whisky as fuel. They raged against a decision to eschew extra time in what they believed was a stage-managed piece of sorcery to create another game and more revenue. The police battled to control the situation and, in the end, 60 people suffered injuries.

Such violence was in contrast to the heroics elsewhere that year. Most startling of all was probably Wentworth Gore's victory in the men's singles championship at Wimbledon at the age of 40. He is the only man of such maturity to have done so and he repeated his success in 1909, aged 41 years, 182 days. That was his third win (he won also in 1901, and he won the doubles once). But he lost the final in 1912, aged 44, against Tony Wilding. In golf,

JH Taylor won the Open for a fourth time, at Deal, in perfect weather and, in rugby union, the touring Australians taught England a few lessons. Their cricketers did too, retaining the Ashes after losing the first Test at Edgbaston with Warren Bardsley, a left-hander, hitting 136 and 130 at The Oval in the final Test to help clinch the series and become the first man to score a century in both innings in a Test match.

Taylor's golfing success drew him level with Harry Vardon and James Braid but, one year later, Braid, a lanky Scot, went one better at St Andrews by securing his fifth win as a new decade began to unfold, an era to be scarred, if not eclipsed, by World War One.

Below: Multiple Open champion, James Braid, won the title five times between 1900-1910.

WELL PLAYED OLD BOY

2

SIGNIFICANT EVENTS, particularly the erection of stadiums, began early in the next decade. England's rugby union headquarters at Twickenham were created and opened in January, when England beat Wales 11-6, their first triumph over them since 1898. The land on which the stadium was built was purchased for just £5,572 12s 6d and was known as 'Billy Williams' cabbage patch' after its previous owner. In February, a football ground was opened at Warwick Road, Old Trafford, for Manchester United. The ground had a billiard room, a gym and tip-up seats in the stands. It also had a capacity for 80,000. Only the best for the Reds, as ever.

England's rugby win over Wales was the springboard to triumph in the enlarged Five Nations championship, their first title since 1892, but such success was not matched by the touring cricket side in South Africa where they were beaten 3-2 despite the magnificent efforts of Jack Hobbs. The sublime batsman of his time, a great fielder and respected man, 'the master', born in Cambridge, set a host of records: 61,237 runs

Right: Jack Hobbs played for Surrey and England from 1905-1934. He was knighted for his services to cricket.

DOROTHEA LAMBERT CHAMBERS – THE QUEEN OF WIMBLEDON

One of the great figures of women's tennis at the turn of the century, Dolly Lambert Chambers, as she was known, won Wimbledon no fewer than seven times. Her first appearance in the final came in 1903, her last 17 years later when she was 41. She holds the record for the fastest Wimbledon final, beating the unfortunate Dora Boothby in just 12 games in 1911.

A vicar's daughter, Dorothea also holds an Olympic gold medal and were it not for the outbreak of the first world war, when Wimbledon was suspended for four years, she would almost certainly have added to her total. She came close in a classic encounter in 1919 when she held two match points against Suzanne Lenglen before the French star clawed out a 10-8, 4-6, 9-7 victory.

She was also beaten by Lenglen in her last appearance in the final. Her last ever match did not take place until 1927 at the age of 48. Following this she retired to concentrate on a career as a professional coach. She later switched to badminton, winning two All England titles.

Yours faithfully
J B Hobbs

SUZANNE LENGLEN AND TENNIS ARTISTRY

If anyone was looking for fashion icons in sport in the early part of the century, they would have been drawn to Suzanne Lenglen. Not only did she start a trend by wearing a bandeau, to keep her hair under control, but she introduced short and pleated skirts and short-sleeved vests. As a result, she moved freely while, often, her opponents struggled against the weight and the restrictions of their heavier old-fashioned uniforms. Born at Compiegne, in France, on May 24, 1899, Suzanne Rachel Flore Lenglen earned her place in British sport's century by dominating Wimbledon from 1919 until her retirement, as an amateur, in 1926. She won both the singles and the doubles every year, except for 1924 when she pulled out with jaundice. Athletic, balletic and charismatic, she attracted crowds and attention like no other before her. After retiring, midway through the 1926 Wimbledon championship, she turned professional and toured in the United States. She died in 1938, aged only 39.

and 197 or 199 centuries (depending on source and interpretation) along with a dependability that saw him exceed 1000 runs for a season 26 times in his career. On the South African tour, alas, his best efforts were not enough. Despite an average of 67.73, he was on a losing side which included the under-arm bowler George Simpson-Hayward, who took 23 wickets.

Understandably, Manchester United were happy in their new Old Trafford home and in 1911 they 'christened' it by lifting the Football League championship, following a 5-1 thrashing of Sunderland. It was their first title win since 1908 and, as ever, provided one of the highlights of a sporting year dominated by such traditional events as CB Fry's batting for Hampshire, Wales' victory in the Five Nations rugby championship, the brilliance of Harry Vardon's golf at Sandwich in the Open and the emergence of one of rugby league's most precocious talents, Harold Wagstaff, who played with such success for Huddersfield.

Wagstaff, signed by the Yorkshire club at the age of 15, became the youngest professional and international in British rugby history as he inspired 'the team of all talents' to three championship wins and three Challenge Cup successes in the war-interrupted decade. Vardon had tied with Arnaud Massy in the Open but showed all his relaxed style and class in the play-off, winning his fifth British Open title out of six, in all, from 1896 to 1913.

In 1912, one of football's now-forgotten, but most significant, rule changes took place. Goalkeepers, previously allowed to handle the ball anywhere in their own half, were restricted to handling only in their own penalty areas. It had no dramatic effect. In Stockholm, at the Olympics, England retained the football title by beating Denmark 4-2 in the final. Only Arthur

Berry and Vivian Goodwood appeared in both the London final, of 1908, and the 1912 final. These Olympics, in Sweden, saw the American-Indian Jim Thorpe win both the decathlon and the pentathlon, a rare and outstanding achievement. Unhappily, he was to be stripped of his medals six months after the games, held in early July, because he had received payment for playing in a minor league baseball game three years earlier. He was to be pardoned, finally and eventually, in 1983, when his medals were returned to his family, 30 years after his death.

In other sporting highlights of 1912, England won an unusual triangular Test cricket series against Australia and South Africa, Tegalie became the first horse to win both the 1000 Guineas and the Derby, the MCC enjoyed a tour of Argentina, described as a 'sporting and social success' and South Africa, including three Luyt brothers, began their tour of Britain with easy victories over Scotland, Wales and Ireland. When the Springboks met England, in January 1913, it was a tougher contest, but they emerged victorious, winning 9-3 at Twickenham.

By the start of the 'teens, other issues were starting to creep into British sport. Not least, political. And particularly feminism. On June 8, a suffragette, Emily Davidson, died from her injuries four days after flinging herself at Anmer, the horse carrying the colours of the

Below: Emily Davidson and Anmer, lie on the track at Epsom.

King of England, during the Derby on Epsom downs. Hotspur, in *The Daily Telegraph*, said 'the most unsatisfactory, sensational, and lamentable Derby in the history of the race was added to the records' as a result. In his description, he wrote that a 'dreadful thing' happened as the horses rounded Tattenham Corner, adding that the jockey, Herbert Jones, lay prostrate after striking the hard ground with his head when flung clear. 'So, too, did the wretched creature who had caused the terrible fall.' In cricket, Sydney Barnes took 49 wickets in four Tests in South Africa on the 1913-14 tour, at an average of 10.93.

All the action, the heroism and the achievements and records built up a swell of interest for the public and established a calendar of events, with a natural seasonal rhythm, which was to remain in place largely unaltered for the rest of the century. The images changed, the clothes, the equipment, the fashions and the photography, of course, but the underlying pattern remained the same. The British sporting public enjoyed knowing what was to happen, where and when, in their lives and much as they roared their approval of great upsets and comebacks, enjoyed them all the more for knowing they took place within the framework of a tradition even as the drum of an impending war could be heard.

Hence, such events as the King's first appearance at an FA Cup final, at Crystal Palace, on April 25, 1914, to see Burnley beat Liverpool by the only goal, in front of 72,000 spectators. Or Miss Cecil Leitch's success in winning the Ladies' golf Open at Hunstanton in a stirring and dramatic final during which she overcame, more than anything, her own highly-strung nature to control her play. Or Dorothea Lambert Chambers' triumph in the Wimbledon singles for the seventh time. All showed that British sport remained in good spirits on the eve of the first world war. The proximity of the carnage was made obvious in Lyons, in July, when six days after the assassination of Archduke Ferdinand, a German driver, Christian Lautenschlager, won the French Grand Prix in a Mercedes. The French crowd were not amused, or appreciative. They did not clap any of the German victors. As they expected, the two countries were at war within a month.

The hostilities did not end all sport in Britain, but severely curtailed it. WG Grace

Left: Cecil Leitch (right) the champion woman golfer of her time.

DICKY OWEN AND WELSH RUGBY

Dicky Owen was a wonderful scrum-half who played a record 35 times for Wales between 1901 and 1912 and also played for Swansea. He played in the Wales team which won the Triple Crown four times. Innovative, clever and popular, he produced the unorthodox pass which helped the Welsh beat the All Blacks in 1905. Later, he became a steelworker and then a licensee. He died, when he took his own life in Swansea, in 1932, aged 55.

NOT OUT, YOUNG MAN!

In his later years, WG Grace became bigger than his reputation, both in girth and as a cricketer. However, after retiring from first class cricket he played on in charity matches in front of huge crowds, eager to see the great man come out to bat. In one such match he came up against a young 20-year-old bowler who was desperate to get the great man out. He hit him with an absolute beauty, second ball, whipping the bails off. Nobody moved except Grace, who bent down, picked up the bail, put it back on the stumps and said: 'Young man, they've come to watch me bat, not to watch you bowl. Please proceed.' The game carried on with Grace batting!

wrote to the *Sportsman* in August and said: 'I think the county cricket season should be closed for it is not fitting at a time like the present that able-bodied men should play and pleasure-seekers look on.' Most sports followed suit. But football, having discussed its position closely with the War Office, decided to continue its championship and cup competitions, but opened its clubs' stadiums on non-match days for recruitment programmes. At one, a poster asked: 'Do you want to be a Chelsea diehard...Then join the 17th battalion of the Middlesex Regiment and follow the lead given by your favourite players.'

Everton duly won the league and Sheffield United the cup, after beating Chelsea in the so-called 'khaki' final at Old Trafford where many troops, some injured, watched from the terraces. After that, most professional sports were virtually brought to a close until the war was over — though there were many famous matches played in the regional wartime

HARRY VARDON – SIX-TIME OPEN CHAMPIONSHIP WINNER

Until Bobby Jones came along, Harry Vardon was considered the greatest golfer in the world, winning six British Opens, the first in 1896, the last in 1914. The overlapping grip is widely believed to have been invented by Vardon although this has long been debated. Whether or not it is true, Vardon was living proof of how smoothly a golf club could be swung.

Born in Jersey, Vardon first played in the Open championship in 1893, finishing in the top 25, and the following year finished fifth. With J.H. Taylor the big name in golf at the time, Vardon still didn't cause much of a stir until, in the spring of 1896, he trounced Taylor in a 36-hole challenge match. Despite this Taylor remained the hot favourite for the 1896 Open at Muirfield, but Vardon was one of six contenders in the final day when he needed to card a 76 to win.

In a sensational finish, Vardon and Taylor tied for victory and came back the next day for a 36-hole play-off. Vardon won it by four shots. That was the start of the so-called Vardon era and he took two of the next three Opens.

In 1900, he embarked on a strenuous tour of the United States, where the sport was beginning to take off, to promote a new ball. He picked up the US Open on the way but could not sustain his mastery over the next three years. That he managed to clinch three more Open championships was remarkable, as was his attempt, in 1920, to win another US Open crown at the age of 50 when he finished second.

CB FRY – THE GREAT ALL-ROUNDER

Tall, handsome, athletic and intellectually gifted, CB Fry's brilliance and versatility marked him out as a unique sportsman at the turn of the century.

He captained England's cricket team six times in 1912 but also played soccer for England and Southampton, for whom he played in the 1902 FA Cup final and, with seemingly no limit to his talent, he set a world long jump record.

His main sport was, of course, cricket in which he had a prolific career. In the 1901 season alone, he scored 3,147 runs including 13 centuries. He was a brilliant conversationalist and stood for Parliament three times as a Liberal although he was never elected. Politics played a crucial role in his life. He was even, at one point, offered the throne of Albania but turned it down. Fry's many commitments prevented him from ever touring Australia but he did just about everything else before retiring from first-class cricket in 1921 after a career of unprecedented sporting and intellectual prowess.

championships around England and on an irregular basis — and some clubs and organisations suffered financial hardship as a result. Arsenal, for example, were reported to be £60,000 in debt by the end.

In 1919, sport returned, but not at full strength. Jack Dempsey won the world heavyweight boxing championship in New York in early July, just as Wimbledon resumed normal service with Gerald Patterson winning the men's singles by outpacing his fellow-Australian Norman Brookes, the holder, who most critics agreed had lost much of his pace since 1914.

In the ladies' tournament, Dorothea Lambert Chambers, the defending champion, also succumbed to younger legs in the shape of Suzanne Lenglen of France, who was to reign supreme in south London until 1926, except for 1924, when she had jaundice and withdrew before her semi-final. In the 1919 final, she played her part in an epic that ended 10-8, 4-6, 9-7 and included the sight of Mlle Lenglen sending for a cognac-soaked sugar lump, supplied by her father, during an interval to revive her flagging spirits. In the Victory Cup, Chelsea, using several 'borrowed' players, beat Fulham 3-0 amid controversy. In Scotland, Celtic beat Rangers to the championship by one point while, in France, Henri Desgrange, the founder of the Tour de France, introduced the idea of the 'maillot jaune' to identify the leader. It was a good idea and it stayed.

By 1920, true signs of sporting recovery could be detected. When the new football season began in August, it was with 66 clubs in three divisions, but in tennis, at Wimbledon at least, it was all the same. Lenglen, only 21, beat Lambert Chambers again, this time 6-3, 6-0. Undoubtedly, one era was ending and another was about to begin.

1920-1929

A SENSE OF ROMANCE

3

AFTER THE WAR, THE SPORT. In the 1920s, people were happy to show their relief from hostilities and the struggle to recover, by embracing sport more passionately than ever before. The patriotism of conflict was transferred into a patriotic love of sporting action as every major sport grew in size, status and organisation and every event attracted seemingly enormous crowds. It was the same all over the world, but in Britain it seemed more intense than anywhere else. Football, cricket, boxing, rugby union and league, golf, motor racing, horse racing and tennis all attracted capacity attendances; but most memorable of all were the crowd scenes at Wembley in 1923 at the 'White Horse' Cup final where a lone mounted policeman did his best to control the hordes who spilt on to the pitch. That famous day, in its way, epitomised British sport of the 1920s, a decade for all kinds of heroes.

White trousers may have remained *de rigeur* at Wimbledon, even with hats and caps; athletes may have run in button-collared vests; footballers wore baggy shorts and played with an often-soaked heavily-laced leather ball, made of panels and covered in mud; golfers

Below: Police try in vain to hold back the crowds who streamed onto the Wembley pitch in 1923.

SIR HENRY SEGRAVE AND THE PURSUIT OF SPEED

Knighted in 1929, for his services to British prestige, Henry Segrave died on Lake Windermere in June 1930 during an attempt at improving the world water speed record, which he had set at 98.76 mph, when his Miss England II hit an underwater obstacle. Born in Baltimore of an Irish father and an American mother, he was the first man to hold both the land and water speed records at the same time, having done the dry stuff in his 23-litre Irving Napier 'Golden Arrow' also in 1929. As a racing driver, he won 31 of his 49 races. Segrave was one of a generation of 'speed kings' along with Donald Campbell who portrayed themselves as men of steel with rigid nerves and cool brains.

JOE DAVIS – THE MAN WHO MADE SNOOKER A WORLD GAME

Born in Whitwell, Derbyshire, on April 15, 1901, Joe Davis was a supreme snooker player whose unrivalled dominance allowed him to remain unbeaten from winning the world snooker title in 1926 until 1955. In that time, he became so vastly superior to his rivals that, after winning the title for the 15th time in 1946, he chose to retire from championship play. Between 1928 and 1965, he put together 687 century breaks. Davis was also the first man to hold both the world snooker and billiards titles simultaneously. He learned to hold a cue and play in his father's public house and he retained the same accomplished ease and confidence throughout his long career. He died in July, 1978, in Hampshire after helping establish himself and his sport as a world game.

wore tweed jackets on cold afternoons; and sports fanatics everywhere breezed with joy in flat caps, top hats, bowler hats and trilbys; futhermore, they still wore cardigans, collars and ties; and most famously, everywhere, everyone seemed to play and watch their sport with a broad smile and a sense of release and pleasure rarely seen before or since. There was a purity in British sport, a sense of romance, that captured the ambience of the inter-war years before widespread professionalism and rampant commercialism arrived and drove it away.

The FA Cup final of 1921 was one match that epitomised this spirit of the age. In the game, Tottenham Hotspur beat Wolverhampton Wanderers 1-0 and lifted the trophy; but, in the ambience of the stadium at Stamford Bridge, the crowd and the players shared something much more rare and refined in the torrential rain. It was recalled, by *The Daily Telegraph*, that 'we saw the real heart of the nation on Saturday — a great, loyal heart .... on a white line that, in a twinkle, was obliterated by a deluge, sudden and rampageous. More than 70,000 people, already on their feet sang, "God

save the King" as some wonderful disciplined choir, then, as with one voice, they broke into deafening cheers.' The quagmire dimmed no one's enjoyment, but reduced the game to a farce. The winning goal, by Jimmy Dimmock, was seen as a fluke since, on a run from the half-way line, he enjoyed a lucky rebound of the ball from a defender's legs and then saw a skidding shot elude the diving goalkeeper.

The following year, 1922, another FA Cup final story was significant. Indeed, so significant that it was repeated *ad nauseum* in the cinemas up and down the country as part of a controversial sports section in the news. Huddersfield, thought to have died as a club two years previously, beat Preston 1-0. The goal was a penalty by Billy Smith, the first to decide a cup final, in the last final to be played at Stamford Bridge. It was also the incident which led to the rules changing to prevent goalkeepers moving on their line (this time, Preston's amateur JF Mitchell was likened to 'an excited monkey on a stick awaiting a bag of peanuts') and the first major trophy won by Herbert Chapman, Huddersfield's manager who went

SEND IN THE NURSE

Melbourne could be a very hostile place for English batsman in the 1920s and during one Ashes series the greats, Jack Hobbs and Herbert Sutcliffe, batted together to make a large stand with which the Aussies were none too pleased. As the runs clocked up and the time passed, the intimidation got worse. The chants echoed: 'Send in the army to shoot them,' and 'send in the fire brigade.' Then a lone voice was heard across the ground: 'Send in nurse Armstrong, she'll get the buggers out,' and the crowd erupted in response — much to the puzzlement of Jack and Herbert. It was later discovered in the England camp that nurse Armstrong was Australia's infamous abortionist.

WILFRED RHODES – CRICKET'S GREATEST ALL-ROUNDER

Not only the oldest, but also the best. Wilfred Rhodes did for cricket's image and reputation what Stanley Matthews did later for football, what WG Grace had started and what few since have been close to emulating. He took more wickets in first-class cricket than anyone else and scored more runs, as an all-rounder, than all but 15 batsmen. In his long career, he was a masterly slow left-arm bowler and a reliable batsman, who graduated from being England's number 10, in 1899, to opening with Jack Hobbs in the period from 1910 to 1920. He completed 16 doubles of 1000 runs and 100 wickets. At Kingston, Jamaica, in 1930, he became the oldest Test player at 52 years and 165 days. He played Test cricket for 31 years, appearing in 58 Test matches from 1899 until 1930.

on to establish himself as one of the greatest in the history of the game with his successes for the Yorkshire club and then Arsenal.

And then came 1923 and the 'White Horse' final, confirmation, if it was needed, that football was the opium of the masses. Who won? Well, actually, Bolton Wanderers beat West Ham United 2-0, a result few cared to remember. The crowd that descended on Wembley that day far exceeded the capacity of the stadium, and the over-spill poured onto the pitch, delaying kick-off for 45 minutes. The lasting image was of a lone policeman on a white horse trying to control the crowd. In reality, these crowd scenes were a forerunner to far more tragic events elsewhere later in the century. But for the Lancashire club from the spinning town, these were glory years — they won the cup in 1923, again in 1926, when they beat Manchester City 1-0, and again in 1929, with a 2-0 victory over Portsmouth in front of a crowd of more than 92,000 at Wembley. If anyone, at this time, could say Wembley was their second home, it was Bolton.

But cup football was not the only mass attraction of the 1920s. Consider these following sporting landmarks of epic proportions and the excitement they caused: a world record crowd of more than 100,000 watched Jack Dempsey knock out Georges Carpentier to win the world heavyweight boxing championship in Jersey City; Burnley went 30 games without defeat on their way to taking the league title by five points; Australia won the Ashes in England in 1921; Sir Henry Segrave became the first Briton to win a Grand Prix when he triumphed in the 1923 French race at Tours; Harold Abrahams won the 100 metres gold medal in the 1924 Paris Olympics, the first sprint victory by an Englishman and a

STEVE DONOGHUE – THE RACING IDOL OF THE 1920s

Born in Warrington, in November, 1884, Steve Donoghue had to go to France and then Ireland, where he was champion in 1908, before he could claim recognition in England. When he did, he became the idol of the racing public of the 1920s and one of those heroic men of sport of his age whose face inspired half the nation. Champion jockey for ten successive years from 1914 to 1923, he rode more than 100 winners in a season five times, peaking at 140 in 1920. He also rode 14 classic winners, including six Derby victors, but his greatest feat was to win the Derby three times in succession from 1921 to 1923. After winning the double of 1000 Guineas and Oaks in 1937, on Exhibitionist, he retired. Courageous, balanced, charming and popular, he was an icon of his time.

ERIC LIDDELL AND THE CHARIOTS OF FIRE

While Harold Abrahams sprinted to British glory in the 1924 Olympic Games, so too did the religious, serious-minded and individual Eric Liddell in his own very different kind of way. The China-born runner, whose father was a missionary in the Far East, could turn out for Scotland as a rugby winger (as he did seven times between 1922 and 1923), but even though he was a great all-round sportsman he was to be remembered as much for what he did outside sport as in it. Most notably, he ran in the 400 metres, not the 100 metres, because the shorter sprint was held on a Sunday; but he could have won that and both the 400 and the 200 if in the mood. As it was, he won the 400 metres gold in an Olympic and European record time of 47.6 seconds which was to stand until 1936. By then, having returned to China in 1925 to work with his father, he had died following two years of internment in a Japanese concentration camp.

Cambridge Blue; in 1925 the offside law, requiring two opponents, instead of three, to be between an attacker and the goal, was introduced in football amid much consternation; one of so many 'invincible' All Blacks teams toured Britain unbeaten and, at Taunton, Jack Hobbs beat WG Grace's record of 126 100s.

The decade's breathless progress on all sporting fronts included, in 1926, the first British Grand Prix at Brooklands, dubbed the 'Ascot of motor racing'; fast bowler Harold Larwood's emergence and first Test for England which came in the second Test of the Ashes series and Herbert Chapman's move from Huddersfield to Arsenal where, apart from gaining unprecedented successes, he earned disapproval for introducing numbered shirts. The pace was unrelenting as Cardiff won the FA Cup in 1927, taking it out of England for the only time with a lucky goal from Hughie Ferguson, whose shot was virtually thrown into his own net by Arsenal's Welsh goalkeeper Dan Lewis; in the north-east, Hughie Gallacher led Newcastle to the title; while on Daytona Beach, in Florida, Major HOD Segrave broke the world land speed record for a mile by travelling at an average of 203.79 mph. At Wimbledon, Helen Wills Moody won the first of her eight titles in 1927.

By 1928, Tottenham Hotspur were relegated, Walter Hagen won his third British Open golf championship, and America's seventh in nine years, and the Wembley

'Wizards', a remarkable Scottish football team (with a famous forward line of three-goal Alex Jackson, Jimmy Dunn, Hughie Gallacher, Alex James and Alan Morton) thrashed England 5-1 at Wembley in front of a record attendance of 80,000 for an international fixture. Great players of huge popularity ruled football in these days when many sportsmen would not dare to have their photograph taken without a cigarette hanging from the corner of their mouth. Men such as George Camsell, who scored 59 goals for Middlesbrough in 1926-27, their promotion season; Wally Hammond, who took a record 78 catches in the season and 10 in one match, for Gloucestershire against Surrey; and then Dixie Dean, who hit 60 the following year for Everton, as they won the league title, were living legends — particularly Dean, 40 of whose goals that season came from headers.

Everywhere the crowds were huge. Everywhere they were perfectly-behaved, not least Newmarket, where the first official Totalisator was introduced in 1929 to universal acclaim. At last, money was loosening up, people were spending it and enjoying life. Perhaps Herbert Chapman had shown them how by paying more than £20,000 for two players — Bolton's David Jack and later Preston's Alex James — to replace one great one who had retired, Charles Buchan. James, the inspiration of the Wembley Wizards, was to prove that, like all great managers building great teams, Chapman knew how to spend a lot of money wisely.

DIXIE DEAN – 60 GOALS IN A SEASON

A footballing legend, a goalscorer of such power and accuracy with his heading, it was said that when he nodded 'good morning' to his opponents, particularly goalkeepers, on the streets of Liverpool, they would instinctively flinch and dive into the gutter. Bernard Joy, the former Arsenal centre-half who later became a football writer, said Dean could leap from standing on to a billiard table. Sir Matt Busby, who played against him in the 1933 FA Cup final, said simply: 'He could out-jump, out-time and out-head any defender.'

Robust, strong, swarthy and beloved by all Liverpudlians, William Ralph Dean was born at Birkenhead in Cheshire on January 21, 1907, and died, on March 1, 1980, in Liverpool after collapsing at Goodison Park after an Everton v Liverpool fixture. For such an icon of his city and his times, there was no other way to go. He began his career at Tranmere Rovers, joined Everton in 1925 and remained with them until 1938, scoring 379 goals in 437 league matches. In 1927-28, he scored a record 60 goals in 39 Football League games. In other competitions, he scored 22 that season. His total of 82 was an inarguable statistic that proved his greatness as a goalscoring talent. For England, he scored 12 goals in his first season, scored in each of his first five games and registered a total of 18 in 16 matches. With Everton, he won the Football League championship in 1928 and 1932 and the FA Cup in 1933.

1930-1939

THE GROWTH OF WORLD SPORT

IF ANY DECADE SAW SPORT spread its wings and fly, it was the 1930s. From the popular foundations of the 1920s, British sport took off in a way that must have been unimaginable to the average spectator. In the age of the General Depression, it was an escape from reality into romance — and everyone loved it. The decade saw growth in every way, but most notably in the quality of the play and in the brilliance of the spectacle in British and international sport.

Football saw the introduction of the World Cup finals, thanks to Frenchman Jules Rimet, and the early excellence — as ever — of the Italians, not to mention the arrival and debut of Stanley Matthews; cricket witnessed the blossoming of Don Bradman, the run-machine and record-breaker, and the controversy over bodyline bowling; the 1936 Olympic Games saw Adolf Hitler upstaged by Jesse Owens; tennis supplied the arrival of Fred Perry who won Wimbledon, a feat not emulated since by

Below: The world's most famous greyhound – Mick the Miller – with his owner, Mrs. Arundel Kempton.

any other British male, and then did it again twice more, a feat not equalled until Bjorn Borg achieved a hat-trick in the 1970s.

Great sportsmen blossomed and everyone tried to play and perform with a real sense of style. This was a special age — of dancing matinee idols, escapism, slicked down hair for men and giggling fun for girls, a time for records and music and fun and heroes. Men like Alex James, Gordon Richards, Ted Drake, Wally Hammond and Owens captured the imagination and so too did four-legged beasts like Mick the Miller, a greyhound to beat the world, Easter Hero, a wonderful jumping horse, and Golden Miller, the only horse to win both the Grand National and Gold Cup during the peak years of National Hunt racing. Sport held up a mirror to life and showed how to overcome all adversity with a smile. But where to begin?

Cricket and football, perhaps, more than

HERBERT CHAPMAN – MANAGER OF VISION WITH AN IRON FIST

As the creator of two teams, at different clubs, which were to win three consecutive English league titles, Herbert Chapman (right) earned a reputation as the greatest football manager of his generation and, perhaps, the finest of all time. Using thorough preparation and deep thought, he raised the art of his job to a new height and delivered, to Huddersfield Town and Arsenal, previously unprecedented successes. His fame and reputation earned him a worthy memorial in the form of a bust in Highbury's marble entrance hall where players of every successive Arsenal generation have stopped and marvelled at his achievements.

Born in January, 1875, in Kiveton Park, a mining village near Sheffield, in Yorkshire, Chapman was the son of an illiterate miner. An intelligent man, he trained as a mining engineer, but signed professional forms as a player for Northampton Town in 1901, and embarked on a playing career that took him to Notts County and Tottenham Hotspur. His managerial success began in 1921 when he joined Huddersfield. He led them to an FA Cup success the following year and in 1924 to the league title — the first of three they won in succession with a team he built, organised and planned.

At Arsenal, he created the country's leading team and club and laid the foundations for traditions which have remained ever since. In his eight years in charge of Arsenal they reached the FA Cup final three times and won the league title twice.

At his funeral, there were huge crowds in Hendon. The pallbearers were David Jack, Eddie Hapgood, Joe Hulme, Jack Lambert, Cliff Bastin and Alex James – the players that made up Arsenal's formidable forward line. He was remembered for the yellow boots he wore as a player, the autocracy of his management style and his innovations: numbered shirts, white balls and floodlights. A modernist and a visionary, Chapman was the manager of the century.

any other sports of the time, drew the biggest crowds and held them rapt. But all over the world sport was in booming good health and, in 1930 alone, Uruguay won the inaugural World Cup finals, on home soil, beating Argentina 4-2 in the final in Montevideo (to where England, Scotland, Ireland and Wales declined to travel and therefore did not participate), and Don Bradman, at only 21, began his sprees. The Australian batsman's runs came during his first Test series in England, in which he scored 974 runs at an average of 139. At Headingley, he hit 309 not out on the second day of the third Test on his way to a world record 334. Even more impressively, he came in when the first wicket fell for just two runs, and the knock included 100 before lunch. In the same year, Bobby Jones did golf's grand slam; the first Commonwealth Games took place, in Canada, with English hurdler Lord Burghley winning three gold medals; and Sir Henry Segrave, having broken the world water speed record, crashed and died in his boat on Lake Windermere.

The FA Cup final at Wembley on April 26, 1930 was the first at which the two teams, Arsenal and Huddersfield, came out side by side. It also saw the Graf Zeppelin airship flying overhead throughout the match. Herbert Chapman, the Arsenal manager, had, of course, been the architect of Huddersfield's triumphant days in the 1920s before moving to London, but he showed no compassion as his new team, inspired by the trickery and quick-thinking of Alex James, won their first honour of consequence to widespread popular acclaim.

GORDON RICHARDS – CHAMPION OF CHAMPIONS ON HORSEBACK

Born on May 5, 1904, at Oakengates, Sir Gordon Richards rode a record 4870 winners and was champion jockey a record 26 times. He was la creme de la creme on the English turf. In his final year, it was announced that he was to become the first English jockey to be knighted, days before he won the Derby at Epsom on Pinza. A strong, determined and somewhat unorthodox jockey, he used a long rein but retained perfect balance and exuded an enormous will to win. He died at Kintbury, in Berkshire, on November 10, 1986.

FRED PERRY – GREATEST BRITISH TENNIS PLAYER OF ALL TIME

Mention Fred Perry and there are no arguments about his place as the outstanding British tennis player of all time. He won eight grand slam tennis titles, including winning Wimbledon three times; and no other Briton has won anything to match since. He was the most stylish, admired and successful man in British sport in the 1930s and his name has remained a byword to sporting excellence since.

Born on May 18, 1909, at Stockport in Cheshire, Frederick John Perry first achieved fame by winning the world table tennis championship in 1929, aged 20. It was a springboard to gain similar success on the tennis courts before going on to turn professional. He travelled to the United States and took part in, and won, the 1933 US Open, beating Wimbledon champion Jack Crawford in five sets. He was the first Briton to win the American title since 1903.

A year later, he won Wimbledon for the first time, beating Crawford again, thus becoming the first British winner in 25 years. Further triumphs followed in 1935 and 1936. He was the first man to win three in succession. Not until Bjorn Borg, 40 years later, was that record to be equalled. He won the American title again at Forest Hills in 1934 and 1936 and won also the 1935 French and the 1934 Australian championships. He was the first player to win all four major titles, but did not hold them concurrently and so missed out on being the first winner of a grand slam.

After 1936, he turned professional and toured. Later he became an American citizen, serving with the US Armed Forces in the second world war. A bust of Perry now adorns the grounds of the All England Club.

Below: The Graf Zeppelin passes over Wembley during the 1930 FA Cup final between Arsenal and Huddersfield.

THE BATTLE OF HIGHBURY

In 1934, Italy won the World Cup and lost the 'Battle of Highbury', a friendly international against England at the Arsenal stadium which was anything but amicable. England led 3-0 at half-time, but struggled to hold their advantage in the second half in the face of a considerable onslaught by their visitors. The Italians resented the rushes, by Ted Drake in particular, at their goalkeeper Carlo Ceresoli when he had possession of the ball — a move which was allowed in England, but then banned on the continent. Also Italy were without their centre-half Luisito Monti from the seventh minute and played with 10 men. The victorious England team suffered: Eddie Hapgood played on with a broken nose, Eric Book had an injured elbow and Drake an injury to his leg. Monti broke his foot.

HERBERT SUTCLIFFE – IMMACULATE AND RELIABLE

The cricketer with the best average of any Englishman against Australia, Herbert Sutcliffe was a smart, tidy and elegant man who was utterly reliable on and off the pitch. Born on November 24, 1894, at Summer Bridge near Harrogate in Yorkshire, he was a prolific opening partner with Jack Hobbs for England and with Percy Holmes for Yorkshire. He was commissioned as a second lieutenant in the first world war and, therefore, did not make his debut as a first-class cricketer until he was 24. But from then on, he scored runs like a machine. By 1932, he was on fire as a batsman. He scored 3336 runs at an average of 74.13 and these efforts included his highest score of 313 for Yorkshire v Essex at Leyton when, with Holmes, he put on a world record 555 for the first wicket. Against Australia, in his Test career of 54 matches, he scored 2751 runs at an average of 66.85. He later became a Test selector and a successful businessman. He died on January 22, 1978, at Crosshills, near Keighley, in Yorkshire.

Top: Wales, on their way to claiming the Five Nations rugby championship, against Ireland at Cardiff in March, 1932.

Above: The England team that took on the Australians during the 1932-33 Ashes tour. The tour will be forever known as the 'Bodyline series'.

Above: Tommy Farr lands a left on Joe Louis during their world title fight in August 1937. Sadly for the Welshman, Louis retained his title on points after 15 rounds.

In rugby league, the Australians were less well-received as, during their tour of Britain, a dispute followed the third Test and marred the series. The Australians demanded a final showdown game which they lost. Such desire to win, almost at all costs, began to creep into sport in different areas. It was an almost-invisible feature which was to have a lasting and irrevocable effect later in the century once professionalism took hold.

In 1931, however, the age was essentially innocent, even if tarnished by sad events such as the death, on September 5, of John Thomson, 22, the Celtic and Scotland goalkeeper, who suffered a severe head injury (a fractured skull) when he was kicked after diving at Sam English's feet during the derby match against Rangers at Ibrox Park. Thomson's death, five hours after the incident, was the first directly attributed to injury in a first-class game. English, barracked mercilessly afterwards yet not blamed for the incident, moved to Liverpool to escape the bigots and later returned to Ireland.

In the same year, America routed Great

SIR HENRY COTTON

The son of an iron founder, Henry Cotton was born into the middle classes in 1907. In a game where the majority of British professionals came from working class backgrounds, Cotton was more suited to amateur golf, where playing excellence bought its own rewards.

Cotton was seen as one of the finest talents within the game from the moment of his first tour appearance. A year after making his Open Championship debut in 1926, a youthful Cotton came to prominence after playing an excellent opening two rounds at St Andrews before finishing eighth. The result prompted him to make winning the title his main aim, despite the American dominance of this era.

However, Cotton buckled within touching distance of the trophy in 1933 having led with 18 holes to play, and a round of 79 ended his hopes of victory. A similar collapse occurred a year later, but after an opening two rounds of 67 and 65, Cotton had already decimated the rest of the field with a tremendous exhibition of strokeplay that showed his growing maturity. Despite a 72 in the penultimate round, his nine-stroke advantage proved enough as he clinched his first Open success whilst suffering stomach cramps during the final round.

A 1937 triumph at Carnoustie brought him his second Open title, regarded as his greatest achievement as he left the whole of the winning United States Ryder Cup team trailing in his wake.

At the time firmly established as the greatest player in the land, Cotton's progress was disrupted by the outbreak of war. Unperturbed, Cotton landed the 1948 Open title at the age of 41 before taking a break from championship golf. His knighthood was announced a few days after his death and his name remains synonymous with the Open Championship.

GOLDEN MILLER AND THE GOLDEN YEARS

In the 1934 Grand National, Golden Miller, ridden by Gerry Wilson, won in a record time of nine minutes and 20.4 seconds. It was historic. The horse was also carrying a top weight of 12 stone and two pounds, but the victory completed a magnificent double of the National and the Cheltenham Gold Cup. The Gold Cup win was the third of five in succession with four different jockeys. Bred in Ireland, Golden Miller was indeed a golden horse. Trained by Basil Briscoe and then by Owen Anthony, Golden Miller won 29 of 55 races and was never a faller between 1930 and 1939. A statue of him was unveiled at Cheltenham in 1989.

TED DRAKE – SEVEN IN ONE AFTERNOON AT VILLA PARK

As a centre-forward, Ted Drake was revered in the 1930s. His great feat was to score all seven goals on Saturday, December 14, 1935, when Arsenal travelled to Aston Villa and won 7-1. But it is less well-known that it was the third time that season that Villa had conceded seven goals at home and were defensively a vulnerable team. Drake's goals at Villa Park equalled the league record for one match; and the previous season, by scoring 42 goals in 41 appearances, he helped Arsenal win the championship and set a record for one season. On his famous day, Arsenal were without Alex James and Joe Hulme and Drake, himself, played with a heavily-strapped knee (he later had a cartilage operation), but every shot went in. 'I was fortunate,' he said. 'Everything I tried seemed to come off.'

Britain in the Ryder Cup at Scioto, in Columbus; West Bromwich Albion beat city rivals Birmingham 2-1 at Wembley, in front of 92,406, to win the FA Cup with the youngest team to appear in the final; and Manchester United, after losing the opening 12 matches of their league campaign, were relegated to Division Two along with Leeds United.

The following year, 1932, Wales won the Five Nations rugby championship, played by only four teams because France were barred for breaching amateur rules. France returned in 1947. In cricket, Australia proved themselves the dominant power by beating South Africa 5-0 in a series which, at Melbourne, featured Bert Ironmonger taking 11 for 24 on a sticky wicket which was ideal for his left-arm bowling. And in Lancashire, a certain footballer called Stanley Matthews made his debut for Stoke City against Bury in a Second Division fixture: not the most auspicious launch of a great career.

By the end of the year, the big story was the one being cabled back from Down Under — England's use of the 'leg theory', otherwise known as 'bodyline' bowling, on their tour of Australia. The tactics were plain: to position a cluster of fielders around the leg side and then bowl a barrage of fast, short-pitched balls at leg-stump, causing the batsman to make a defensive stroke, or duck out of the way for his own safety. It was highly controversial. Questions were asked in Parliament in England and Australia and the names of Harold Larwood, Bill Voce and Douglas Jardine (the bowlers) were to be forever tarred by the infamy of the day. England won the series, but a battling Bradman still managed to average 56.57.

In 1933, Wally Hammond scored 336 not out in his final innings on tour in New Zealand; Gordon Richards rode 259 winners, thus

DOUGLAS JARDINE AND THE BODYLINE CONTROVERSY

On the cigarette cards of the day, it read simply D.R. Jardine (Surrey). He had an open face and steady, gazing eyes, fair hair receding at the temples and the cool look of someone capable of making the toughest decisions. He did. As Douglas Jardine, captain of England, he became the most universally unpopular cricket captain in his lifetime and all because of the bodyline tour to Australia in 1932-33 when he encouraged his fast bowlers to follow the 'leg theory' and bowl on a line which saw the ball pitch and rise towards the batsman's ribs, shoulders or throat. The tactic of bowling on the 'bodyline' caused great alarm to the Australians and matters came to a head in Adelaide in the third Test when the South Australian crowd became so alarmed at what was happening that they threatened to invade the field. Mounted police were called.

According to EW Swanton, the long-serving cricket correspondent of *The Daily Telegraph*, the 'bodyline' tactics were discussed and agreed upon by the players before they left England. Harold Larwood and his Nottinghamshire fast-bowling partner Bill Voce had used similarly intimidating bowling tactics before, but without the 'umbrella' field introduced by Jardine in Australia. Even Bradman was curtailed. His average fell from 139 in England to 56 and the Ashes were won back 4-1 by England in the series.

Despite his infamous association with the 1932-33 Ashes, Jardine was also a notable middle order batsman with classic technique who averaged 48 runs in his 22 Tests for a total of 1296. Born in Bombay, India, in October, 1900, he played for Winchester, Oxford University and Surrey. He died in Montreux, Switzerland, in June 1958.

breaking a 48-year record of 246 held by Fred Archer; and Fred Perry, once just a table tennis player, emerged from the small game to lead England to Davis Cup victory. Richards' success heralded the receipt of a congratulatory telegram from the King of England's private secretary as he stood, it was reported, surrounded by his boisterous colleagues and beaming with pleasure.

The following year, Jack Hobbs hit his 197th and last first-class century, Golden Miller won the Grand National and the Cheltenham Gold Cup and Italy, on home soil, won the World Cup, beating Czechoslovakia 2-1 in Rome in the final.

Uruguay, the first champions, did not travel from Latin America to defend their crown and Italy's dictator Benito Mussolini claimed their win was a triumph for fascism. Almost unnoticed, but not quite, Australia travelled to England for a cricket series and regained the Ashes — following their loss in the 'bodyline' series — by winning 2-1. In the fifth and final Test at The Oval, Don Bradman and Bill Ponsford put on a record stand of 451 for the second wicket in just 316 minutes. The record stood for 57 years.

In football, 1934 saw Arsenal win their second successive league title under the guidance of Herbert Chapman, who died of pneumonia in January, alas, before the season was over. Worse still for this supreme innovator, he was not to know that the same team would, in 1935, go on and complete a hat-trick of successive championship triumphs and that in one match, against Aston Villa, Ted Drake would score seven goals to equal the record for the First Division set by James Ross of Preston North End in 1888. Arsenal's success is noted widely. In 1927, the London club was the venue for the first broadcast of sport on radio; in 1936, it was to be the first to host television cameras when Everton visited. Technology, in the media, was on the march.

But goalscoring feats were also becoming commonplace. Drake had hit 42 goals in Arsenal's championship campaign the previous

WALLY HAMMOND

Renowned as a majestic craftsman who mastered all the best Test bowling in the world, Wally Hammond is regarded as one of the finest batsmen in history. With balanced assurance and steely concentration, his powerful striking off the back-foot and perfect sideways-on action, Hammond helped himself to a plethora of mighty scores.

But the supreme talent of the man ensured that he excelled in other areas too. A fast-medium bowler, he possessed shrewd control and late swing, accompanied by a menacing desire to increase his speed at will. A considerable haul of 83 Test wickets, combined with his outstanding reputation as a nimble outfielder or devastating slip catcher, made him one of the greatest all-rounders to set foot on a cricket pitch.

Born in Dover in 1903 and the son of a soldier, he spent his childhood in China and Malta before his family returned to England. He went to school in Gloucestershire because he didn't want to play for Kent, and despite having to serve a two-year qualifying ban, Hammond went on to star for his adopted county.

A formidable total of more than 50,000 runs, including more than 7,000 runs and 22 centuries in 85 Test matches, highlighted the prolific nature of Hammond's scoring; a high score of 336 in 318 pulsating minutes against New Zealand in 1932-33 included ten sixes and cemented his position as the scourge of Test bowlers throughout the world.

SIR LEN HUTTON

Leonard Hutton maintained his position at the top of English cricket from an early age, and in 1938, when aged just 22, he broke Don Bradman's world Test record by scoring 364 against Australia at The Oval. The innings lasted over 13 hours.

His famous knock was one of 19 centuries for England, and he captained his country in 23 Tests, of which they lost only four without conceding a series. This impressive record was achieved after a war-time operation which left him with one arm shorter than the other. But, despite this handicap, his considerable natural prowess as a cultured hitter shone through.

In the 1950-51 Ashes series, when England were defeated 4-1 by a rampant Australian side, Hutton averaged 88.83, 50 more than any other England batsman. Indeed, the strength of the England batting order at this time was relatively weak, and it was left to Hutton and Denis Compton to become the mainstays of the side.

winter, but even that was bettered in the 1935-36 season when Robert 'Bunny' Bell scored nine goals on Boxing Day for Tranmere Rovers in a Third Division North match against Oldham in a record 13-4 victory, 24 hours after Oldham had won 4-1 on Christmas Day. Bell hit 33 for the season, but this was small fry compared to the feats of Joe Payne for Luton Town. Overlooked and regarded as reserve wing-half, he was called up due to an injury crisis for their Third Division South clash with Bristol Rovers on April 13, 1936, and, after a dull and slow opening 20 minutes, scored 10 goals from all angles in a 12-0 victory. The following campaign, he hit 55 goals as Luton marched to promotion.

Speaking of marching, the Olympic Games of 1936 featured plenty of stage-managed stuff for Hitler's benefit, but even his best-laid plans could not upset the inspiring athleticism of Jesse Owens, a black American who ran into folklore and legend by winning four gold medals in Berlin.

Curiously, Great Britain won the Olympic ice hockey title for the only time in the winter games in Garmisch-Partenkirchen.

In 1937, Hampden Park played host to a British record crowd of 149,547 spectators

PRINCE ALEXANDER OBOLENSKY

The most famous of all the tries at Twickenham, England's hallowed rugby home, was scored by a 'Russian prince'. Prince Alexander Obolensky, the son of an officer in the Czar's Imperial Horse Guards, came to England as a baby to escape the turmoil of the Russian revolution.

After making a name for himself as a sprinter at Trent College, Obolensky moved to Oxford and became a right winger with electric pace in the Varsity matches of the thirties. Throughout the Depression, Obolensky fuelled his pace with a habit of eating a dozen oysters before taking the field for any match in the London area. After three years at Oxford, Obolensky went on to play for England and in January 1936, against the All Blacks, his eccentric nature came up trumps on the rugby field.

The English backs were attacking to the right, and aware of the fact that the All Blacks were covering that side of the field, the Russian Prince, without the ball, turned inwards, took a short pass, and raced diagonally left as he wrong-footed the startled New Zealanders who were unable to match his explosive run. This amazing effort added to an earlier score, when he raced 40 yards to round the All Blacks' full-back on his way to an easy try.

Sadly, Obolensky's career, which included spells with Rosslyn Park and the Barbarians, ended in tragedy when he became the first rugby international to lose his life in the second world war. Serving in the RAF, the jovial Obolensky had joked to team-mate Arthur Rees that he 'couldn't get the hang of landing'. On a black day in March 1940, Obolensky was killed as he attempted to land his fighter after a training flight near Ipswich.

(plus, it is believed, another 10,000 who crept in free of charge) as Scotland beat England 3-1 in a Home International Championship meeting. Wales took the title for the last time, some compensation for their boxer Tommy Farr's failed effort to beat Joe Louis and win the world heavyweight boxing championship on August 31, when his family and friends crowded around their wireless radios to hear commentary in the early hours from Madison Square Garden. Farr lost on points.

By 1938, the rumble of distant guns was heard and European and British sport began to prepare itself for another war. England's footballers, on an end of season tour in Berlin, were forced to give the Nazi salute when the German anthem was played, but still beat their hosts 4-2. When Aston Villa played a friendly the following day, they refused to do likewise and were jeered by the crowd throughout the game.

But life went on and Don Budge, a tall American tennis player, managed to achieve arguably the most difficult Grand Slam of all by taking the Australian, French, Wimbledon and American titles in the same year without the aid of air travel. Also, in 1938, Helen Wills Moody won her eighth Wimbledon singles title, 11 years after her first and Len Hutton, at just 22, struck an Ashes record 364 in the final Test, at The Oval, on a day when Don Bradman was carried off the field with a fractured shin. England declared with an amazing total of 903 for seven. Hutton's innings lasted for 13 hours and 20 minutes.

The late 1930s saw also a rapid growth in interest in motor racing. In 1935, the first Donington Grand Prix was staged and won by Richard Shuttleworth in an Alfa Romeo P3 Monoposto. Two years later, it earned serious international status and attracted the big Hitler-backed manufacturers from Germany — Mercedes and Auto-Union. In October, 1938, the race was won by Tazio Nuvolari, leading the Auto-Union team, in front of 61,000 spectators. By 1939, however, the second world war brought such frivolity to an end. Sport was to take second place again and nothing made this more apparent, after another summer of Wimbledon domination by Americans, than the plight of the touring New Zealand rugby league team. They arrived in late August and within three days were to learn that Hitler's German troops had invaded Poland. One day after their opening match — a victory over St Helens — war was declared. After their second, a win against Dewsbury, they took the long ship home.

ALF GOVER AND THE CALL OF NATURE

Alf Gover, who bowled for England in the 1930s, remembers touring with Douglas Jardine in India when, on the eve of a match, 'Delhi belly' knocked out a number of England players, including himself. On the morning of the game, the team was just able to muster 11 men, if not all fully-fit. Jardine said he would bat if he won the toss to give the wounded a chance to heal. However, he lost it and the team had to field. Gover marked out his run as the umpire threw him the new ball, then set off. When he reached the wicket, however, he did not deliver the ball but kept on running past the startled batsman, between the slips and up the pavilion steps into the dressing room. Five minutes later, a bemused Jardine followed. 'Gover, Gover, where are you?' he inquired. 'In here sir,' came the distant reply. 'Where's here?' quizzed Jardine further. 'In the toilet sir, I have had an accident,' said Gover. 'That's all very well, but can we have the ball back?' demanded Jardine, 'We want to start the match!'

1940-1949

WAR AND RECOVERY

WAR, AGAIN, brought sport to a standstill. But not forever. After an initial decision to halt as much activity as possible, the public view changed from one of condemnation of anything that could dilute the military effort to one which saw sport as an aid to morale and fitness. Football, as the most popular of the mass spectator sports, reflected these views most clearly. The Football League and the FA Cup were suspended, but a range of other competitions, organised on a more local basis, ensured that games continued to take place and that the crowds were entertained. Top professional players were, of course, called up by the services and their presence was used as a form of positive propaganda, lifting spirits and encouraging positive thinking. Anything he can do, we can do. So the soldiers believed as they began their workouts in vests and shorts.

Hence, Tommy Lawton became a physical training instructor, Ted Drake and Sam Bartram took on defensive duties and Cliff Bastin spent his wartime as an ARP warden in London, manning a lookout in a lofty position at Highbury, an occupation which enabled him to continue to turn out for Arsenal, and keep fit, in his spare time. According to *The Sunday Times Illustrated History of Football* Bastin, famously, was claimed by the Italians broadcasting on Rome Radio, to have been captured and held as a prisoner of war. In the circumstances, it was little more than a poor piece of propaganda-spreading which failed. Bastin had, ironically, not been passed fit enough for active service because he was slightly deaf and, reportedly, getting worse.

Drake and Bartram, meanwhile, were widely photographed in British newspapers wearing uniforms and carrying rifles, with bayonets fixed, over their shoulders. According

ALEC BEDSER AND THE LEG-CUTTER

His debut may have been delayed by the war, but once he was given his chance Alec Bedser certainly took it with both hands. Bedser, born in Reading on July 4, 1918, made his Test debut against India in 1946 and responded by taking 24 wickets at 12.41 in three matches, including 7-49 and 4-96 on his opening outing. For the following eight years, he provided a consistent service as a bowler with his in-swing bowling and a very effective leg-cutter.

In 1953, he began with 7-55 and 7-44 against Australia at Trent Bridge, took 39 wickets in the series of five Tests and established a record of wickets in a Test career which he enlarged to 236 in 51 Tests by 1955. Then came the new tyros like Frank Tyson, Brian Statham and Fred Trueman and Bedser's day was past. He went on to become an England Test selector and was chairman of the selectors for 13 years from 1969 to 1981.

to the captions, they were 'somewhere on the east coast.'

There were complaints from some that the footballers had an easier time in the army than others. If true, it was for a good reason. If they were allowed to continue to play football, it was because their skills not only helped their army or other services teams play well, but also they raised the morale of the people around them and, quite often, on the other team. According to one report, one 17-year-old boy whose last match before joining the navy was for his local choir school found himself, in his next fixture (for a navy unit team and a visiting RAF side) lining up against Stanley Matthews.

Such experiences were commonplace. Before the retreat from Dunkirk, an army team, captained by Stan Cullis, and including Denis Compton, Wilf Copping, Tommy Lawton, Joe Mercer and Bert Sproston, played against a French international side in three games. During the D-Day landings, one group of soldiers enjoyed an impromptu game on a beach, but had to abandon it because one of the goals exploded. All this gives some idea of the enthusiasm which was maintained for football wherever it could be played, even in battledress.

Back home, meanwhile, with the closure of the Football League, 10 regional leagues were organised and clubs were allowed to use guest players to replace anyone away on National Service. Some teams were entirely bereft of

DENIS COMPTON – THE BRYLCREEM BOY

Born in Hendon, London, on May 23, 1918, Denis Charles Scott Compton was the first cricketing cavalier to cash in on his commercial value. He won his county cap with Middlesex at only 18 and became the youngest player to score 1000 runs in his debut season. One year later, he was in the England Test team. In 1938, he scored his maiden test century, against Australia. He went on to play 78 Tests in all up to 1957 and, but for the war and dodgy knees, would have played many more. He also played football for Arsenal and won a league championship medal in 1948 and an FA Cup winner's medal in 1950.

His deeds were those of a comic strip hero and he was treated as one when he advertised Brylcreem and became as famous for his dashing looks and image as for his sporting prowess. His partnership with Bill Edrich, for Middlesex and to a lesser degree for England, was equally famous. They played together from 1937 to 1957 and scored runs upon runs: Edrich hit 36,965 and Compton hit 38,942. In the *Wisden* of 1948, RC Robertson-Glasgow wrote: 'Compton has genius and, if he knows it, he doesn't care. Edrich has talent; or, more truly, he started with a number of talents and has increased them into riches.' They were known as the Middlesex Twins, an ideal partnership of courage and flair. But neither lived into old age. Edrich died, aged only 70, following a fall. Compton died on St George's Day, 1997, aged 77, and Westminster Abbey was filled for his Thanksgiving Service.

STANLEY MATTHEWS – FOOTBALLER OF THE YEAR

In 1948, the Football Writers' Association introduced a new idea: the Footballer of the Year. The first winner was Stanley Matthews, the brilliant English winger regarded as the 'wizard of dribble' whose career was to become synonymous with the post-war growth and success of English football. Matthews was also the first European Footballer of the Year in 1956, the first player to win the CBE in 1957 and the first footballer to be knighted, in 1965. He made his debut for Stoke City, aged 17, but did not retire until he was 50. He moved to Blackpool in 1947, inspired them to reach the FA Cup final in 1948, when they lost 4-2 to Manchester United, and went on to make 54 England appearances between the ages of 19 and 41. He returned to Stoke in the final stages of his career before retiring.

players and, therefore, fielded all-guest outfits. A League Cup was also run, in which guest players were not allowed. Some international matches continued, but mostly these were representative games to raise money for the Red Cross. The standard of play was variable, depending on who was available. But the sport, at least, carried on with the support of Winston Churchill who demonstrated his estimation of its value by attending an England v Scotland fixture in 1941 and meeting the two teams. Seven members of the war cabinet attended the game.

Cricket also continued with many charity matches, and two popular teams, the British Empire and the London Counties XI, toured the country playing against village sides to raise money. The Empire team was mostly amateurs with a few additional celebrities while the London team was mostly professionals. The circumstances of the cricket matches were often extraordinary and combined teams became commonplace. In one Bank Holiday fixture at Lord's, Middlesex and Essex played Kent and Surrey in front of 22,000 spectators. These were the origins of one-day cricket.

But in Australia, at least in 1939-40, life continued as normal. Robert Menzies, the Prime Minister, said it would help morale stay high. Don Bradman was at his peak. In nine matches, he scored a total of 1,475 runs at an average of 122.9. The following year, however, it all ended following the Japanese assault on Pearl Harbour. From then on, many of the best Australian cricketers were to be seen performing in the military teams in England — such as the Australian Imperial Forces and the Royal Australian Air Force. When they combined to play in the summer of 1945, between the VE-Day and the VJ-Day, they provided the entertainment known as the Victory Tests. Despite the presence of such men as Walter Hammond and Len Hutton, they were not recognised officially.

Opposite top: from left to right, Joe Mercer, Matt Busby and Don Welsh prepare for war in 1939.

Opposite: British Army sides were common during the second world war. This one, from 1942, featured Stanley Matthews (front row left).

STAN MORTENSEN – GOALS GALORE FOR BLACKPOOL AND ENGLAND

Sometimes forgotten or overshadowed by Stanley Matthews, Stan Mortensen scored four goals for England on his debut against Portugal in May 1947, on the day before his 26th birthday. In his England career, he made 25 appearances and hit 23 goals, including England's irst World Cup goal, against Chile, in 1950. In the 1953 FA Cup final — forever afterwards known as the Matthews final — he scored a hat-trick as Blackpool beat Bolton 4-3. His treble was the first at Wembley in a final. A fine player, with a good eye for goal and a natural athleticism allied to great skill, he was a man whose achievements were never measured to their full glory because he was also the lesser of the two Stans — Matthews and Mortensen.

JOE MERCER

After returning home from World War One, Joe Mercer's father took a football out of his kit-bag and threw it to his four-year-old son. From that day on, Mercer would be obsessed with the game. Born in Ellesmere Port in 1914, Mercer was one of soccer's great characters. He was a hugely successful player, with glory coming at Everton and Arsenal, where as captain, he helped his side win a glittering array of honours, including the 1948 and 1953 championship titles.

As a manager, Mercer tasted success with Aston Villa. At Manchester City, he created a side of true quality and skill, bringing the glory days back to Maine Road, winning the First Division title in 1968 and the FA Cup a year later. After bringing his magical flair to Coventry City, Mercer put the fun back into international football as he took over as England caretaker-boss in May 1974.

Various sports continued to flicker throughout, erratically adding some statistics to their history books. In snooker, for example, Joe Davis recorded his 14th victory in the world championship in 1940. In 1946 he won it for the 15th time and promptly retired. His brother Fred then took on the responsibilities and lifted the crown himself in 1949 and again, from 1951 to 1956. Horse racing also managed to maintain a credible thread of continuity with the Derby, notably, running at Newmarket rather than at Epsom. Bill Nevett, known as the 'cock of the north' rode three winners in the war years — Owen Tudor, in 1941, Ocean Swell, in 1944 and Dante, in 1945. In rugby league, Leeds won the 1941 Challenge Cup when they beat Halifax. In 1942, the same

Above: During the second world war, Tom Finney fought with the Tank Regiment in the Eighth army, and then returned to the only club he played for — Preston North End — and his job as a plumber.

Below: The Moscow Dynamos take to the field against Chelsea, during a tour of Britain in 1945.

Above: An inspector gives war-time instructions to cricket stars Leslie and Denis Compton (right).

Opposite: Denis Compton and Bill Edrich of Middlesex toss for 'ends' at the start of a charity cricket match at Highbury in 1949.

STANLEY ROUS – REFEREE AND FIFA PRESIDENT

One of the most influential men in the history of international football, Stanley Ford Rous was born on April 25, 1895. He trained as a teacher, became a successful referee in charge of 34 international matches in Europe between 1920 and 1934, when he became secretary of the English Football Association. In 1961, he became the president of FIFA and remained in that position until he retired in 1974. He was awarded the CBE in 1943 and was knighted in 1949. He died in Suffolk in July, 1986.

teams reached the final. Leeds won again. In boxing, Jackie Paterson won the world flyweight championship in 1943, when he knocked out Peter Kane in Glasgow, in the first round.

When the war ended, there was a natural sense of release, freedom and celebration and these emotions were felt everywhere. In sport, the same sensations were shared. In October, 1945, the Moscow Dynamos arrived in Britain. They were acclaimed. In their first fixture, against Chelsea, they gave their opponents each a bunch of flowers. The match ended in a 3-3 draw. Next, Cardiff City were beaten 10-1, Arsenal (despite the inclusion of Stan Mortensen and Stanley Matthews) were beaten 4-3 and Rangers were held to a 2-2 draw.

They were skilful, artistic and thrilling to watch — the perfect antidote to the war games and around 250,000 people turned out to enjoy their ability. Indeed, their tour signalled not just

1
2
TOTAL
WICKETS

the end of the war, but the beginning of something else: a new era of fevered celebration of sport, the great escape, for some, from the numbing reality of everyday living in the aftermath of the second world war. New stars emerged. New dreams were born. And, sadly, the old heroes of the pre-war years were just that now — old heroes of another, bygone, time.

Widespread bomb damage, pavilions and dressing rooms boarded up, injured men and women — and craters where, once, there were wickets; after the war, it was no straightforward task for sport to kick off again. The great stars of the late 1930s were much older. Many had retired and gone. Some continued. But little seemed the same. It was a time of repair and transition everywhere, in sport as in life. But, once again, as in the 1920s, sport as entertainment became the opium of the masses as they sought escape in the union of excitement triggered by the thrills of competition.

Right: Donald Bradman, the scourge of English cricket, retired in 1948.

TOMMY LAWTON

It is never an easy task taking over from a legend but Tommy Lawton is one footballer who managed it when he replaced Dixie Dean at Everton. Lawton's name is still talked of in hushed, revered tones. Hardly surprising: four days after his 17th birthday he became the youngest player ever to score a league hat-trick. That was at Burnley but it was at Everton where, in the last two pre-war seasons, Tommy really made his mark. He was top scorer in both those seasons, winning a League Championship medal in 1939 in the process. After the war, he signed for Chelsea where he stayed for two years before moving on to Notts County. At the time, they were in the Third Division but that didn't prevent Lawton winning the last four of 23 international caps for England during which time he scored a remarkable 22 goals. Lawton went on to represent Brentford, Arsenal and Kettering Town before entering management.

So, the 1940s saw bankruptcy, financial struggles, unexpected results, sad retirements and tragedies, such as the disaster at Burnden Park, Bolton, in March 1946, when barriers collapsed during Bolton Wanderers' FA Cup tie against Stoke City and 33 people died. It was the worst tragedy in the history of football at that time.

Yet, below the surface, there were stirrings of another kind in sport. The impact of the wars and the evolution of air travel meant that international fixtures became more common, a wider variety of people took part, stars with a different kind of breeding and background emerged. Sport, as a whole, shifted out of the predictable social orbits in which it had lived previously and spread itself more widely through the population.

When Wimbledon re-opened for business in June, 1946, a total of 32 nations were represented and John Olliff, in *The Daily Telegraph*, remarked that it was 'the most tangible and poignant symbol of peace,' adding that the 'thirty-two nations of widely differing colours and creeds' had come to London 'to contend for the highest honours in the game.' He noted one player in particular, Jadwiga Jedzrejowska, who came from Warsaw via Berlin, who had not practised, who had no tennis clothes or shoes. She had not touched a racquet in Poland at all during the war, he reported. 'She is thinner and obviously wearied and worn by her country's sufferings. Her obvious joy at being back once again at Wimbledon is shared by all the competitors from European countries ravaged by the Nazis.' In this, one Polish girl embodied the feelings of a multitude of enthusiasts as life and sport began to return to normal.

The sufferings also added to the depth of feeling and the determination to achieve excellence on the field. Many men and women touched new heights in quality and effort. Their work brought light to the dark world of repair and recovery. Stanley Matthews, arguably the most dedicated footballer in the history of the game, emerged as a great player of extraordinary dribbling skills; Denis Compton and Bill Edrich revealed that controlled and elegant cricket could also be glamorous; the Olympic games came to London, in 1948; Don Bradman called it a day; and a young football manager, called Matt Busby, took over at Manchester United, without a major trophy since the first world war, heavily in debt and forced to ground-share with Manchester City at Maine Road.

Busby, formerly a Manchester City player,

RANGERS WIN FIRST TREBLE

After struggling in the group stage, when they recovered from a poor start to qualify for the last eight at the expense of Glasgow rivals Celtic, Rangers put themselves in prime position to achieve a historic first domestic treble success when they defeated Raith Rovers 2-0 in the League Cup final in March. A 4-1 defeat of Clyde after strolling through the tournament gave the Blue half of Glasgow a triumph in the Scottish Cup, their second trophy of the season, but the League proved to be their toughest hurdle.

Two days after that Cup success, a 1-0 win at Morton gave them a single-point advantage over Dundee in the race for the title. However, on the following Wednesday, Dundee leap-frogged back to the top and it was all down to the final Saturday of a tense campaign.

Rangers went to Coatbridge and a Willie Thornton hat-trick helped them to a 4-1 victory over Albion Rovers. Now it was all on the game at Falkirk where the pressure was on Dundee to get over the winning line. Alas, the pressure told and the Rangers faithful were left to salute their treble-winning heroes – a truly, magnificent achievement.

THE IMPORTANT THING IN
THE OLYMPIC GAMES IS NOT
WINNING BUT TAKING PART.
THE ESSENTIAL THING IN
LIFE IS NOT CONQUERING
BUT FIGHTING WELL.
BARON de COUBERTIN

showed a flair for the job that was to transform his new club. Inside three years, they won the FA Cup. In the following decade, the 1950s, they went on to win the league championship three times and lay the foundations of greatness that were to see United win the European Cup, under Busby, in 1968 and, later in the century, rise again and repeat that feat in 1999. But Busby was not the only famous newcomer of 1945. Brian Bevan, a famous Australian rugby league player, made his debut for Warrington and began a career that was to bring him 740 tries. This, like Busby's recovery of United, was a sign of the shrinking world and the determination of ordinary sporting folk in the post-war years.

In 1946, at Bolton, came the tragedy which

Left: Freddie Mills holds aloft his lucky horseshoe after wresting the world light heavyweight title from Gus Lesnevich in 1948, at the second attempt.

Opposite: The opening ceremony of the 1948 London Olympics.

KARL MULLEN – HOOKER AND CAPTAIN OF THE LIONS

Karl Daniel Mullen (left) was born on November 26, 1926, at Courttown Harbour, County Wexford, in Ireland. He was an oustanding hooker who won 25 consecutive Irish caps after bursting onto the international scene after the second world war. He captained Ireland, aged only 21, in 1948 and led them that year to the Grand Slam. In 1950, he led the British Lions on tour to Australia and New Zealand where, despite achieving only one draw, they established themselves as the most popular tourists in living memory.

led to all-ticket fixtures for the most attractive matches. The 1946-47 English league season was characterised, more than anything, by a severe winter which turned the season into one of the longest on record. So many pitches were white with snow that red paint was used to mark the lines.

And, in a shot at the vacant light heavyweight boxing title, came disappointment for gallant Freddie Mills who lost to American Gus Lesnevich, who felled him eight times in 10 rounds of brutal and ferocious punching. Mills came back to win the title from him two years later, avenging his earlier beating, in another grisly fight at White City. But his life ended sadly. He was found dead from mysterious gunshot wounds in 1965.

Among the new English sporting heroes, Stan Mortensen, Tommy Lawton and Denis Compton were three who stood out. In 1947, the former two established their credentials for greatness when they shared eight of England's goals (Tom Finney and Stan Matthews scored the others) in a 10-0 thrashing of Portugal; in another notable football match, a Great Britain team played the rest of Europe and won 6-1 with three goals from Wilf Mannion at Hampden Park, Glasgow, in front of 135,000;

Below: Fanny Blankers-Koen (right) wins the 80 metres hurdles.

and in the same summer, a landmark season for the 'Brylcreem boy', Compton scored 3816 including 18 centuries and averaged 94 against South Africa in a series in which he scored 753, including six centuries.

Compton's record-breaking season of centuries enabled him to pass Jack Hobbs' old record of 16. The same year saw Walter Hammond play his last Test for England, against New Zealand in Christchurch, on March 24, when he scored 79 runs. He was the first man to score 6000 and 7000 runs in Test cricket and the first to take 100 catches as a fielder.

Twelve months later, the spotlight was firmly on London as the capital hosted the Olympics at Wembley where Dutch housewife, Fanny Blankers-Koen, a 30-year-old mother of two, sprinted to glory by winning four memorable gold medals in the 100 metres, 200 metres, 80 metres hurdles and 4x100 metres relay. The stadium hosted 70,000 spectators. Television claimed 500,000 viewers for the opening ceremony. Busby's United came from behind twice to beat Blackpool 4-2 in the FA Cup final (a familiar tale of heroics) and Don Bradman played his last Test, being bowled second ball after an emotional walk to the crease. He first-class average was 99.94 runs. And, in America, Babe Ruth died, aged 53.

In 1949, Brian Close entered English international cricket as the youngest Test player; the 'Brown Bomber' Joe Louis retired from boxing after 25 successful defences of his world heavyweight title; Juan-Manuel Fangio began his motor racing career in Europe (he was to become a familiar victor in England and in races involving Stirling Moss) and the English cricket team won two of the closest cricket Test matches of all time, one by a leg bye on the last ball.

In the FA Cup, Yeovil, of the Southern League, inspired by the crafty scheming of Alec Stock, their player-manager, produced one of the greatest giant-killing feats of all time, defeating Sunderland's 'Bank of England' team, all £60,000 worth of them, 2-1 in Somerset to become the first non-league club to reach the fifth round. There, alas, they were drawn to visit the holders, Manchester United, at Maine Road where they were beaten 8-0. 'We just felt numb,' said Stock. 'But then we heard that our share of the gate (more than £7,000) was more than our entire receipts for the previous season. Suddenly, what had happened on the field was of no significance.'

FRANK SWIFT

The Munich air disaster, while claiming several footballers' lives, also sent the profession of journalism into mourning. Frank was working for the *Sunday Empire News* when he lost his life at the age of 44. He was, unlike so many of today's scribes, an established player, before moving into writing. He was Mancunian through and through, yet it was with the blue half of the city that he made his name as a goalkeeper. After making his first-team debut in 1933, he didn't miss a match for the next five years, making 192 consecutive league appearances. He picked up an FA Cup winner's medal in 1934 and a league championship medal three years later. Yet it was not until 1947 that he won the first of his 19 international caps. The following year Swift became the first goalkeeper to captain England. Many feel he would have won more honours had the war not intervened.

THE STUFF OF LEGENDS

6

AAA
41

IT CAME LIKE A SWELLING SEA, wave upon wave of action and excitement, with an ever-increasing number of spectators drawn in by the fantasy and the revelry of British sport as it gathered unprecedented momentum in a decade of growth and spectacle. Sport, for more people than ever before, became an important part of their lives. It commanded news coverage. It became professionalised on a more serious level. The men who were heroes became stars, even legends. Names like Roger Bannister and Stanley Matthews were to be as common on the front pages of newspapers as the back. Television arrived, too, and took sport with it into the sitting rooms of the nation. Weekends were never to be the same again.

It was the era of the arrival of big time sport par excellence. Sport moved out of the age of pure amateurism, shrugged off its garden fete atmosphere and commercialised its major occasions. The 1950s saw the World Cup in Brazil, the inaugural Formula One world championship races, the Helsinki Olympics, the first tennis Grand Slam by a woman, the breaking of the four-minute mile barrier, further World Cups of real note in Switzerland and Sweden, Jim Laker's world record turn of 19 wickets in a Test match, major European transfers in football with John Charles leading the way by moving to Juventus, and Billy Wright winning a record 100 caps for England.

Just a glance at the appearances of the stars, the teams, their kit, the cars and the facilities from 1950 to 1960 shows the rapid way in which British sport developed in the decade. It was not only the Formula One machines which became

Right: The formidable Welsh rugby side of the 1950s.

ARTHUR ROWE AND SPURS' PUSH-AND-RUN CHAMPIONS OF 1951

Having gained promotion with a short-passing style of play that was to beguile both their fans and their opponents, Tottenham Hotspur maintained the tactic in the First Division in 1950-51 despite criticism and cynicism from their rivals. The style was the creation of their coach Arthur Rowe (pictured here with Spurs winger, Tommy Harner) who believed in three-man triangles of combination play. It was best explained to his players, he revealed, during a train journey back from an away match, through the use of sugar cubes. He spread the cubes around the table to show why his team's last-minute winning goal had been so brilliant. 'I spread the sugar out to map the moves,' he said. 'There were seven passes starting from our penalty area. I argued that if we could play like that, instead of just hoping for something to happen, we would score more often.' In November, 1950, Newcastle United travelled south to White Hart Lane and, after conceding four goals in the first half, ended up letting in seven. Spurs won eight games in succession that autumn and won the first championship title in their history in April with a match in hand.

STIRLING MOSS – CHAMPION WITHOUT A TITLE

He never won a world championship, but Stirling Moss was universally regarded as the finest driver and unluckiest man not to do so. Born in West Kensington, London, on September 17, 1929, he won 16 of his 66 Grands Prix between 1951 and 1961 and was runner-up to Juan-Manuel Fangio each season from 1955 to 1957.

In 1958, he was pipped to the title by fellow-Briton Mike Hawthorn by a point. After several years with less-competitive British teams, Moss joined Mercedes in 1955 as number two to Fangio. He became the first Englishman to win the British Grand Prix that summer, but was never certain that Fangio did not ease off to concede the race. In 1955, he was also the first Englishman to win the famous Mille Miglia sportscar race in Italy. In 1962, he was injured seriously in a crash at Goodwood.

CLIFF MORGAN AND THE REVIVAL OF THE RED DRAGON'S FIRE

In the 1950s, Cliff Morgan was at the heart of everything good about Welsh rugby, which season after season used to strike fear into the opposition. Morgan, more recently a respected television and radio commentator and journalist, was one of the finest fly-halves in the history of the game who was at his best when partnering Cardiff club-mate Rex Willis. Morgan was instrumental in Wales' emotional 1952 Grand Slam success and on the British Lions tour of South Africa three years later scored a brilliant try that paved the way for a classic victory. Between 1951 and 1958 he won 29 caps and still holds the record as the most capped Welsh fly-half. He was awarded the OBE in 1977.

more streamlined. Everything did. And, with the evolution, there was rapid progress in performance which the new media made sure everyone knew about.

But the first great shock of the time was perhaps the biggest story of the fifties too: England's decision to travel to Brazil for the World Cup finals where they met the United States, regarded as one of the minnows of world soccer, and lost 1-0. An Argentine-born player Gaetjens scored the only goal. The result was regarded as one of the greatest upsets of all time, particularly as the England team included such famed players as Alf Ramsey, Billy Wright, Tom Finney and Stan Mortensen. For Ramsey, it left a bitter taste which he used to fire his determination and his ambition — and 16 years later, as manager of England, he was to satisfy his craving by leading them as manager to World Cup success at Wembley.

The early 1950s was also a golden era for rugby in Wales. A young and developing team in red shirts won the Grand Slam and then went on to claim five more championships as well as beat the All Blacks (always a mighty team in any decade) in 1953. English cricket languished and

A PLAYER'S WORD IS HIS BOND

If fate had panned out differently, Tom Finney could have been the first English superstar in Italian football instead of opting for the inhospitable climes of northern England. In 1952, Finney was approached by the wealthy chairman of the major Italian club Palermo, and offered a fortune to play in the then equivalent of Serie A. A villa, a car and £200 a week would have put him into the millionaire's league. Tom was interested and approached the Preston chairman to seek his approval. 'Finney, if you go to Italy, you will never play in England again,' came the reply. 'We have your contract, that is the end of it.' And it was.

struggled with the spin of Sonny Ramadhin in particular as he helped West Indies to a comfortable series victory. Partnering Alf Valentine, he mesmerised the England batsmen. In the winter, a fully-representative British Lions team toured Down Under and won in Australia, but lost in New Zealand. Truly, international sport had arrived.

In 1951, while Oxford University suffered the indignity of sinking in the boat race against Cambridge, Juan-Manuel Fangio clinched his first world championship in a season which saw the inaugural European Grand Prix held at Silverstone, the cars swerving around bales of straw at corners. This first race was held on May 13 and won, not by the great Argentine, but by Giuseppe Farina, a 44-year-old Italian who had been coaxed out of retirement, driving an Alfa

MIKE HAWTHORN – THE FIRST BRITISH WORLD MOTOR RACING CHAMPION

With his looks and style, Mike Hawthorn was the quintessential British gentleman racing driver of his day. Fair-haired, often photographed smoking a pipe, he had an image that was to stay with the public long after his premature death.

Born in Mexborough on April 10, 1929, he died aged only 29 when he crashed his Jaguar road car on the 'Hog's Back' near Guildford, in Surrey, hitting a lorry and a tree. He trained as an engineer, began racing with a Hillman Imp (his father had a garage) in 1951 and moved on up through the ranks.

In his first Grand Prix, he was fourth at Spa in a Cooper-Bristol. In 1953, in a Ferrari, he won the French Grand Prix at Reims and finished fourth in the world championship.

In 1954, he was third but his father was killed in a road accident that threw a shadow over his successes. In 1958, he won the world title for Ferrari before retiring. In his Grand Prix career, Hawthorn won only three of his 45 races, between 1952 and 1958, but left behind a reputation and image that has outlived his achievements. 'Mike Hawthorn was the most colourful and unpredictable personality in post-war motor racing ... a big, flaxen-haired young Englishman with the courage and skill of a champion,' said *The Daily Telegraph's* WA McKenzie.

THE MYSTERY OF DEVON LOCH

One daily newspaper described the Queen Mother's failure to win the 1956 Grand National with Devon Loch as 'the greatest hard luck story in the history of racing.' With 50 yards to go and leading comfortably, Devon Loch suddenly and inexplicably slipped and fell and was unable to continue. The true cause of Devon Loch's disaster is still uncertain. Some have argued that he tried to jump a fence that wasn't there, others that he was startled by the roar of the crowd. Jockey Dick Francis was completely distraught while the horse's trainer, Peter Cazalet, who had prepared the horse to perfection to win the greatest prize in the sport, was devastated. One could only guess the feelings of the Queen Mother who watched the race with her daughters, Elizabeth and Margaret. Few Nationals have ever taken up so many column inches over so many days. To this day, what happened to Devon Loch remains one of racing's great mysteries.

THE MUNICH AIR DISASTER

Twenty-one people, including seven players and three officials from Manchester United, died following an accident at Munich airport on Thursday, February 6, 1958, when a British European Airways Elizabethan airliner, carrying the party back home from Belgrade after a European cup tie, crashed while making its third attempt to take off in a snowstorm late in the afternoon.

Matt Busby, the manager, and eight players were taken to hospital; Busby, in a critical condition, was in an oxygen tent. The chartered plane was carrying 44 people, 11 of them sportswriters. The former England goalkeeper Frank Swift – a guest of the team — died in hospital. Harder still for the families, friends and fans to bear, the great Manchester United player of this Busby Babes team, Duncan Edwards, died two weeks later from his injuries, taking the total to 22. Jackie Blanchflower and Johnny Berry survived, but never played again. Busby, also, survived and guided United to glory.

Opposite top: Alf Ramsey (left) watches in horror as Bert Williams is beaten by a shot from Gaetjens during England's 1-0 defeat by the United States in 1950.

Romeo. He took pole position, recorded the fastest lap and triumphed. But, a week later, in Monte Carlo, Fangio won the Monaco Grand Prix to prove his talent was the one to dazzle.

In boxing, this was the year of Randolph Turpin who overcame the legendary Sugar Ray Robinson, in front of his own fans at Earls Court, to win the world middleweight championship, while in golf, Max Faulkner won the British Open and became the only man to win the title in a tournament played off the mainland at Royal Portrush. In cricket, Peter May made his Test debut for England with a century against South Africa at Leeds. Newcastle, thanks to two goals from Jackie Milburn, won the FA Cup final against Blackpool.

The following year saw some famous debuts and deeds. Fred Trueman played for England, his fast bowling ripping into the Indians at Headingley, and Cliff Morgan, a brilliant Welsh rugby player, inspired his country to another Grand Slam. The Helsinki Olympics were lit up by the 29-year-old Czechoslovak, Emil Zatopek, who won three long distance gold medals in the 5000 metres and 10000 metres (which he had also won in 1948) and the marathon.

In 1953, the fabulous feel of British sport

intensified noticeably. Gordon Richards won his first and only Derby, and Stanley Matthews collected a winners' medal at last with Blackpool for his part in their dramatic 4-3 defeat of Bolton. He laid on goals for Mortensen and Perry in the final minutes as his team recovered from trailing 3-1 to win. Meanwhile, Wales beat the All Blacks 13-8, England regained the Ashes against Australia after almost 19 years, in a famous match at The Oval in which Trueman, Bedser, Laker and Lock were the outstanding bowlers and the 'twins', Bill Edrich and Denis Compton took care of the batting.

Hungary, inspired by Ferenc Puskas, thrashed England at Wembley 6-3. It was a turning point, a watershed, for English football and marked also Alf Ramsey's last international cap as a player. In Vienna, in May, England overcame Austria 3-2 in front of many British soldiers with a late goal from Nat Lofthouse, later dubbed the 'Lion of Vienna'. His heroics were in contrast to the sadness surrounding the career of Derek Dooley, 23, Sheffield Wednesday's centre-forward, who collided with Preston's goalkeeper during a game, broke his leg, suffered the setting in of gangrene and had the limb amputated. He had scored 46 goals in 30 games the previous season to help Wednesday gain promotion.

In motor racing, Mike Hawthorn, aged only 24, ended the 23-race dominance of Italians and Argentines by winning the French Grand Prix for Ferrari. At Wimbledon, Maureen 'Little Mo' Connolly won the second of her three successive ladies' singles titles. Each big story, it seemed, was to be followed by another. Every mountain climbed led to the discovery of a higher peak of success and drama. All were scaled.

So, in 1954, Roger Bannister broke the four-minute mile barrier at Oxford; Jim Peters strove heroically to win the marathon in the Empire

JACKIE MILBURN – THE TYNESIDE TERROR

John Edward Thompson Milburn was affectionately known by the Newcastle United faithful as 'Wor Jackie'. Idolised by the St. James' Park fans, in an era of truly great English centre-forwards, Milburn was recognized as one of the best. He possessed devastating pace and a lethal shot in either foot.

Noted for his spectacular goals, Milburn scored in every round of Newcastle's 1951 FA Cup run, and his fondness for twisting and turning in tight situations made him a legend on Tyneside.

After joining Newcastle United as a youngster during the war, Milburn worked as a pit apprentice before starting his first-team career on the right-wing. His supreme ability paid dividends on the international scene, too, scoring 10 goals in 13 appearances for England.

After scoring a record 177 league goals for Newcastle, Milburn moved to Northern Ireland where he hit more than 100 goals in two seasons for Linfield, before taking up a career in journalism in later life, when he continued his love affair with his beloved United.

Milburn was the founder member of a famous footballing clan, which also included two other famous North-Easterners, the Charlton brothers. But Tyneside continues to remember their favourite son with a statue which stands in the city's main thoroughfare.

JIM LAKER – THE RECORD BREAKING SPIN KING

The rain-affected fourth Test match of an Ashes series at Old Trafford, Manchester in June 1956 was the setting for the greatest one-man bowling performance in cricketing history. Jim Laker, a 34-year-old spin bowler, had already taken an amazing 10 wickets for 88 runs playing for Surrey, as they became the first county to beat the Aussies for 44 years.

This time he was playing for England who, needing a victory to secure the series, amassed 459 in their first innings before the tourists came in to bat. On an unpredictable wicket, Laker and his partner Tony Lock emerged wicketless in their first spell and decided to swap ends. Laker quickly grabbed the first two wickets before Lock reduced Australia to 62 for three.

Eight runs later, Laker had spun his way through the batting order, ending the innings with 9 for 37 as the Australians were forced to follow on. The majority of the next two days were washed out and the visitors came into the final day on 84 for 1, leaving them a fine opportunity to save the match.

But wickets tumbled throughout the day as Laker got into his rhythm, and with just one hour to go, he had repeated his earlier feat of defeating nine batsman in an innings. In his 36th over, Laker bowled to tail-ender Maddox who shuffled his pads to block the incoming delivery. The umpire agreed with Laker's hearty appeal for leg before and the series was won. Laker had spun his way into cricketing legend.

Games, but collapsed 11 times on the final lap; and West Germany, for the first time, won the World Cup by beating the favourites Hungary in Berne. Lester Piggott, at 18 and still living at home, also lost his jockey licence for six months for an incident during the King Edward VII Stakes at Ascot where, it was alleged, he veered to the left on Never Say Die.

In 1955, Newcastle again won the FA Cup, England triumphed 3-1 in the Ashes series Down Under and, at the Le Mans 24-Hours race in France, 83 people died and 100 were injured when Pierre Levegh's burning Mercedes Benz car flew into the crowd after an accident involving

Left: Jackie Blanchflower, the Manchester United centre-half, survived the Munich air disaster but he never played again.

ENGLAND 3 HUNGARY 6 – WEMBLEY 1953

England's shock 1-0 defeat against the United States in the 1950 World Cup in Brazil three years earlier was hard to bear for most supporters, but at least their near-invincibility in the safe confines of Wembley Stadium was unlikely to be threatened. Or so they thought. A visit by the 'Magical Magyars' of Hungary onto the hallowed turf changed all that, as England were soundly beaten by six goals to three on November 25, 1953.

The watching public marvelled at this unknown team from afar, with the likes of Jozsef Bozsik, a brilliant right-half, and the immensely gifted inside-forward combination of Nandor Hidegkuti, Sandor Kocsis and, of course, Ferenc Puskas. They were a trio laden with finesse and dazzling wizardry who scored 210 goals in a 48-match spell in which they lost only once. Unfortunately for the home side, six of that total helped the Hungarians to become the first continental team to defeat England on the latter's home soil.

Mike Hawthorn's car. It was the worst disaster in motor racing history and caused the French government to suspend the sport in France and Mercedes to withdraw. Yet, despite the tragedy in the early stages of the event, the race continued for another 20 hours. Hawthorn won.

In the same year, Alberto Ascari died after a crash at Monza, having survived an accident at Monaco where his car flew into the harbour. Ascari held the record for the highest number of consecutive Grands Prix wins — nine — from June 1952 to June 1953. Stirling Moss provided some British cheer by winning the British Grand Prix at Aintree in front of a record crowd of 125,000. He was the first British driver to win the event. In motor cycling, Geoff Duke won the world 500-cc title for the third consecutive time on a Gilera and

TOM FINNEY – PRESTON'S LOYAL AND PROLIFIC STRIKER

At the peak of his career, Tom Finney was spoken of in much the same way as Stanley Matthews. He could play with equal ease on the right or left flank and, late in his career, even proved to be an accomplished centre-forward. In all he scored 187 goals in 433 games for Preston and was twice voted Footballer of the Year. Sadly, domestic honours eluded him. The closest he got was the 1954 FA Cup final when Preston lost 3-2 to West Bromwich and 1957-8 when they finished runners-up to Wolves in the league.

For England, Finney was as prolific as he was for Preston, scoring 30 goals in 76 games in a 12-year international career. The late Bill Shankly used to say that Finney would have been great in any team, in any era, in any match 'even if he had been wearing an overcoat.'

RANDOLPH TURPIN – THE FLAWED BOXING MAESTRO

One of the greatest fighters Britain has ever produced, Randolph Adolphus Turpin oozed natural flair and a love of the high life. Sadly, his love of the latter meant that he faded from the boxing scene all too quickly, but his undoubted talent shone through in a memorable fight against the great Sugar Ray Robinson in 1951.

Robinson, regarded as almost unbeatable since turning professional eleven years before, had lost only one fight in his career, against the great Jake La Motta, a decision he avenged just a few months before the Turpin fight, as he regained his middleweight crown.

Fighting on home turf at Earls Court, Turpin excelled in front of 18,000 screaming Britons to out-point a shell-shocked Robinson with a masterful piece of strategic tactics. However, just 64 days later, a hastily arranged rematch in New York saw a gallant Turpin edge the first three-quarters of the fight before being knocked off his feet with a left hook in the 10th round.

Turpin staggered to his feet at the count of 10, but the referee Ruby Goldstein stepped in 30 seconds later to halt the fight amid protests from the British camp. Although Robinson went on to enjoy another 10 years at the top, Turpin failed to capitalise on his talent and drifted from the sport.

piloted the introduction of one-piece leathers into the sport.

On the football field, Duncan Edwards, of Manchester United, became the youngest England player of the century to date when he played against Scotland at Wembley aged 18 years and 183 days. He died in the Munich air disaster three years later.

In 1956, at Aintree, came the sort of extraordinary and mysterious drama that was to make Dick Francis famous. This, however, was not of his writing. He was the jockey. Riding Devon Loch, the Queen Mother's horse, he failed to finish when his mount collapsed less than 100 yards from the finish. It was an amazing sight.

By now, television was broadcasting news of all such events and people everywhere were quick

TRAIN MADNESS

Travelling with a Premiership Football Club today is more likely to be by air than by road — by rail is almost unheard of. But things were very different for Stanley Matthews in 1952. Following a poor performance and a home defeat by Aston Villa, Matthews and his Blackpool team-mates were expecting a serious dressing-down before their next match against Cardiff at Ninian Park, especially as their manager Joe Smith told them he had something vital to say. They were left on tenterhooks all week, until finally on the morning of the match, Smith stormed in to the dressing-room and slammed the door. Hush descended. Then the manager spoke: 'Now lads don't forget it is vital that we catch the five o'clock train home' he said. 'So, at the end of the game don't bother having a shower, just get dressed so we don't miss it.' And with that he walked out.

to learn of the latest happenings. The Postmaster General, on behalf of the British Government, thus drew up a list of British sports events which were to remain free from the clutches of any exclusive television arrangements made by either the BBC or ITV (the first sign of political involvement in televised sport). The list included the Grand National, the Derby, the English and Scottish FA Cup finals, cricket Test matches and the Empire and Olympic Games when held in Britain. That meant, at the time, that Gordon Pirie's performances that year were free and up-for-grabs in modern television-speak, as he took a slice off the 5000 metres world record and picked up a silver medal in the Olympics.

In another event that was to become and

Left: Stanley Matthews holds his 1953 FA Cup winners' medal aloft. The match will be forever known as the 'Matthews Final'.

LESTER PIGGOTT – THE JOCKEY JUGGERNAUT

As 'The Chase' stormed home to win at a flat meeting at Haydock Park in 1948, its 13-year-old jockey was blissfully unaware of the future successes he would achieve in a riding career spanning 45 years. Lester Piggott amassed more than 5,300 winners worldwide, including 4,450 in Britain.

Piggott rode a record 30 classic winners between 1954 and 1992, including an unprecedented nine in Britain's showpiece flat race, the Derby. From Never Say Die in 1954 to Teenoso in 1983, his name was synonymous with the race, even though his grandfather Ernest was a triple Grand National winner!

A somewhat withdrawn character, mainly due to his partial deafness and speech impediment, his marvellous balance and perfect judgement made him the finest horseman the country has ever produced. A prison sentence for tax fraud in 1987 failed to dampen Piggott's enthusiasm and desire for riding winners, and he bounced back triumphantly to ride Rodrigo de Triano to victory in the 2000 Guineas at the age of 56.

remain a national institution, the FA Cup final, one of the great stories of the century unfolded as Bert Trautmann, who suffered a broken neck while diving at the feet of Peter Murphy in the opening 20 minutes, played on unwittingly for the rest of the game despite the injury. The post-match X-rays showed nothing wrong, but three days later he was in such intense pain that he checked into the Manchester Royal Infirmary where he was told he had cracked the second vertebra in his neck in two and was lucky to be alive. Originally a German prisoner of war, Trautmann had stayed on to become one of the great personalities of the English game once he had overcome early prejudices against him. In the final, Manchester City, inspired by Don Revie, beat Birmingham 3-1 and Trautmann's heroics earned him the award as the 1956 Footballer of the Year.

In the same summer, Tony Lock became famous in a small way by taking one wicket against Australia at Old Trafford. His success prevented Jim Laker from taking them all in both innings. Laker took 19. The following year, Sugar Ray Robinson won the world middleweight title for a fourth time, and Peter May and Colin

ROGER BANNISTER BREAKS THE FOUR-MINUTE MILE

It happened at Oxford's Iffley Road on May 6, 1954. Roger Bannister, 25, ran a mile in less than four minutes. It was a feat that became one of the most celebrated in the history of British sport, and drew a crowd of more than 2,000 spectators. He was timed, officially, in running the distance in three minutes and 59.4 seconds. This was two seconds quicker than Gundar Haeff's world record, set in 1945.

Bannister's achievement took the world by surprise. Several well-known athletes and trained runners wanted to beat the clock and produce an 'even time' mile that summer, but were beaten to it. Bannister's name will forever be remembered for that mile even though, six weeks later, the Australian John Landy improved the record by trimming it to 3:57.9. Later, in a race known as the 'mile of the century', at the Empire Games in Vancouver, Bannister beat Landy. He ran 3:58.8 and Landy ran 3:59.6. It was the first time two men had beaten four minutes in a race. Bannister, who went on to break a series of other records, was awarded the CBE in 1955 and later became a distinguished neurologist. He was knighted in 1975.

Cowdrey scored a record 411 for England in their partnership against the West Indies.

Althea Gibson won the ladies' singles at Wimbledon, the first black champion to do so and England, with winger Peter Jackson scoring three tries, won the Grand Slam for the first time in 29 years. Significantly, too, after some arguments, Manchester United chose to ignore the advice of the Football League and, instead, entered the European Cup. 'The European challenge should be met, not avoided,' said Matt Busby. In their first game, United beat Anderlecht of Belgium 10-0. They were knocked out by Real Madrid, the holders, who went on to beat Fiorentina in the final.

JACKIE BLANCHFLOWER – FOOTBALLER AND PRIZE-FIGHTER

One of those who survived the fateful Munich air crash was Jackie Blanchflower. He never played again and died in September 1998, 40 years later. As a player, Blanchflower had a reputation for being able to look after himself, and to supplement his meagre income from football, he would earn as much as he could from illegal prize boxing matches in pubs in and around Yorkshire.

One morning in training, his coach Jimmy Murphy noticed a 'shiner' and enquired how he got it. 'Got knocked in training yesterday,' Blanchflower replied and the matter was dropped. Two weeks later, in another fight, Blanchflower's face again took some punishment. This time after training Murphy suggested to Blanchflower that perhaps Matt Busby might like to see him if his face got injured in training again. Jackie took the point and his pugilistic career came to an abrupt end.

Above: The tries of Peter Jackson – the Coventry and England winger – helped England to the 1957 Grand Slam, their first victory in 29 years.

In 1958, at Munich, Manchester United's team of 'Busby Babes' perished in a terrible plane crash on the runway. Ironically, the same year saw the arrival of Pele who, as a 17-year-old prodigy, scored twice as Brazil beat Sweden 5-2 to win the World Cup in Stockholm. In the Formula One world championship, with Fangio retired after winning a record five world titles, it was a vintage British season with Mike Hawthorn outscoring Stirling Moss by a point to take the title for Ferrari. In tennis, Christine Truman defeated Althea Gibson to lead Britain to their first Wightman Cup success since 1930

NAT LOFTHOUSE – THE LION OF VIENNA

The phrase 'traditional, old-fashioned centre-forward' is used to describe many players in the modern era, but it originally derived from the attributes of a working-class, Bolton forward who was nicknamed the 'Lion of Vienna' in his prime. Nat Lofthouse was the archetypal human battering ram who thought of crashing into burly goalkeepers as an occupational hazard.

Hailing from a coal miner's background, Lofthouse was filled with aggression and courage, backed up with prodigious strength and endeavour which helped him plunder a prolific 30 goals in 33 appearances in an England shirt. However, he was much more than a workhorse striker and he was widely revered within the game as a humble man who loved his profession.

A controversial second goal in Bolton's 2-0 win over a Manchester United side ravaged by the Munich air disaster in the 1958 FA Cup Final, when he forced the goalkeeper over the goal-line, is one of the most memorable goals in English football history.

while in athletics, in Sweden, Herb Elliott lowered his own 1500 metres record by two full seconds to 3.36 minutes.

As the decade drew towards a close, the combined might of Trueman and Statham's bowling was proving irresistible as they helped England hammer India 5-0 in a Test series in 1959. During the same summer, in a significant appointment, Bill Shankly took over as manager of the second division club Liverpool, and Hanif Mohammad, having batted for almost 11 hours, was run out for 499, the highest score in first-class cricket. Mike Hawthorn, a dashing hero of the decade, debonair and cravated, with pipe and grin, died after crashing his Jaguar on the Guildford by-pass and Maria Bueno became the first Brazilian woman to win at Wimbledon when she lifted the ladies' singles title. In the 1959 FA Cup final, Nottingham Forest beat Luton Town 2-1 despite playing two-thirds of the game with 10 men following a broken leg suffered by their right-winger Roy Dwight, uncle of Elton John.

1960-1969

SPORT IN FASHION

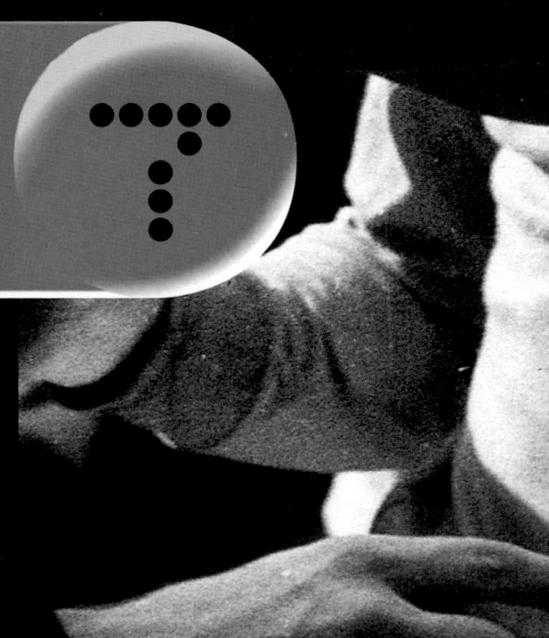

7

AND SO TO THE SWINGING SIXTIES, the decade when sport went pop, when players became celebrities and when George Best became El Beatle. The tidal wave of momentum from the fifties continued, but the atmosphere changed and British sport moved, like television, from monochrome to colour. Air travel shrunk the world as surely as the speed of the media brought home the impact of every competitor's efforts, records and feats around the globe.

Any great sportsman could become a major star almost overnight. It was an age when the gentlemen-sportsmen of the earlier days were overtaken, usurped and replaced by a different band as the old-fashioned working class boys rose up, in music, the performing arts, the cinema, literature and sport, not to mention government, and took control. It was not a revolution, but it was a markedly notable and rocky era of evolution.

As in the 1950s, the events and the deeds came thicker and faster than ever before. All grew bigger and more important by the day. Every sport made a big impact now. Not only football and cricket, but also motor racing, cycling and golf. Every sport had stars to steal the headlines. And that is what they did. From Francis Chichester, in sailing his Gypsy Moth across the Atlantic single-handed in 1960, to Tony Jacklin, who in 1969 became the first Briton to win the British Open since 1951. In between, so many stars were born that the world of sport was a galaxy of twinkling lights.

But where to begin? In football, perhaps, always a good way to measure a sporting pulse. On Wednesday, May 18, 1960, those who were present at Hampden Park in Glasgow saw one of the finest football matches ever played. It was the European Cup final between Real

Below: The Spurs double-winning team of 1961.

FRED TRUEMAN – THE FEARSOME YORKSHIRE TERRIER

Those who know Fred Trueman only from his radio commentaries and his lamentations about the modern game may question his influence on English cricket. They would be wrong. Trueman's out-swinger was responsible for many of his 307 Test wickets, starting on middle-and-leg and making the batsman play. He also had a legendary off-cutter which won the Headingley Test of 1961 and featured in a spell of five for nought.

Trueman was aggression personified, mixed with an artfulness that confused many an opponent. His alleged beer-swilling was slightly unjust, but he certainly was the master of the 'sledging' of the day, full of gestures and comments. He was quick with a fiery temperament which often got him into trouble, not least on the 1953-54 tour of the West Indies. His actions cost him his place against Australia the following winter. He enjoyed his best series in 1963 when he had lost some of his pace but was still a menace with swing, taking 11 West Indian wickets in one Test and 12 in another. He liked to think he was the best bowler ever and that was probably true at the time he retired. Others have achieved more since, however.

Above: Jimmy Hill was instrumental in achieving the abolition of the maximum wage for footballers during the 1960-61 season.

Madrid, the holders, and Eintracht Frankfurt. The result was a 7-3 victory for the Spanish club in a game of such brilliance, it has remained a talking point ever since. The Germans were a very good, tough and determined team. They took the lead. They fought for everything. But Madrid had Ferenc Puskas, Francisco Gento and Alfredo di Stefano, a trio to match any in the history of the game. The 130,000 present can never have seen anything better.

The 1960-61 season began with the mighty Tottenham Hotspur team winning their first 11 successive games on the way towards winning the league championship in what was to be a momentous season for them, as they also won the FA Cup. It was the first English 'double' success since Aston Villa in 1897. Spurs won 31 of their 42 games and played with a swagger that was worthy of the Arthur Rowe philosophy continued by Bill Nicholson. On the field, Danny Blanchflower was an inspirational captain, Dave Mackay a dynamo

JIMMY GREAVES – THE CLINICAL MARKSMAN

In a sensational career, Jimmy Greaves was to top the First Division goal-scoring charts six times with an accuracy and composure in tight situations that marked him out as one of the great strikers of all time. Right place, right time was the key to Jimmy's success, frequently wrong-footing the keeper with clever disguise. A clinical finisher, he relied, as top strikers often do, on excellent service. The fact that he played in the great Spurs side of the 1960s after joining from AC Milan paid dividends.

Famously, Alf Ramsey left him out of England's 1966 World Cup-winning team, believing Greaves was purely a goalscorer who made no other significant contribution to the team. It was a decision that still rankles with Greaves.

Nonetheless he played 57 times for England scoring a remarkable 44 goals. Equally prolific with Chelsea and Spurs, he finished his career with West Ham, who signed him in exchange for Martin Peters. Greaves hadn't lost his skill but his appetite was waning and he was later engulfed by a number of personal problems from which, admirably, he recovered to become a household name in the media.

TEAMTALK

The Busby Babes should also be called 'Murphy's Men' after Sir Matt's number two Jimmy Murphy, who also managed the Welsh national team in his career. He was a reknowned motivator and not afraid to speak his mind. One famous team talk in the 1950s when Wales beat West Germany was reported to have gone along the lines of: 'These Germans were bombing your mums and dads a few years ago. Now go out and get them!'

and John White an elusive genius.

More significantly, however, the same season saw the abolition of the maximum wage for footballers, the 'slavery contracts' according to those professionals who had been restricted to earning £20 a week during the season. The English game was said to be only days away from a national strike when the issues were resolved in the Football League's dispute with the Professional Footballers' Association. Led by Jimmy Hill, the PFA chairman, the players won their breakthrough on January 9 in the wages issue and then confirmed their freedom when George Eastham, who wanted to move from Newcastle to Arsenal, challenged his contract in the High Court and won.

All this change had several effects. At Fulham, Johnny Haynes was made the first £100-a-week player in England, a deal which kept him in London; but others left for the lure of the lire. Joe Baker joined Torino from Hibernian, Denis Law followed from Manchester City for £100,000, Jimmy Greaves left Chelsea for AC Milan for £80,000 and Gerry Hitchens joined Internazionale for the same fee.

Greaves, famously, did not settle and he returned to England later in 1961 and, for a transfer fee of £99,999, was signed by Tottenham Hotspur. His goalscoring genius had

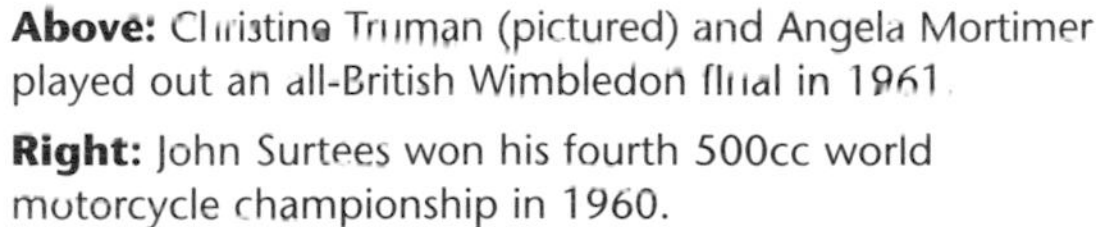

Above: Christine Truman (pictured) and Angela Mortimer played out an all-British Wimbledon final in 1961.

Right: John Surtees won his fourth 500cc world motorcycle championship in 1960.

THE CHARLTON BROTHERS

Jack and Sir Bobby Charlton engraved their names in British sport folklore with their charismatic charm as well as their achievements and dedication to football in long established careers on and off the field. The brothers, hailing from Ashington in the north east, both played in the 1966 England World Cup-winning side. Jack was a strong centre-half, who benefited from the guidance of his club manager at Leeds and national coach Sir Alf Ramsey. Bobby, a man who always talked down his own ability, possessed the guile and expertise to threaten any defence. Bobby, the younger of the pair by just over two years, was equally strong with his right or left foot.

Without doubt one of sport's greatest ambassadors, Sir Bobby Charlton won 106 caps for England during which he scored a record 49 goals. His career with Manchester United included League and Cup wins, but was probably topped at Wembley again in 1968 with two goals in the victorious European Cup clash against Benfica. Following their careers as players, Jack went on to manage the Republic of Ireland national squad whom he helped to unprecedented success by leading them to two World Cups in 1990 and 1994.

been confirmed at Wembley in April, 1961, when he scored one of the record six hat-tricks he delivered for England in their 9-3 drubbing of Scotland. No wonder the Beatles were singing about money as well as love. It was the age of good times for the British sportsman... and not only in football.

In tennis, in 1961, Wimbledon was treated to an all-British final between Christine Truman

Above: Henry Cooper floors Cassius Clay in round four of their world heavyweight title fight in 1963. Clay went on to win in five rounds.

and the victorious Angela Mortimer while, in motor cycling, Mike Hailwood, following in the wheelmarks of John Surtees — who in 1960 had reeled off his fourth 500cc world title — became the world 250cc champion. In cricket, Richie Benaud of Australia made his name by

THE CALL TO ARMS OF COLIN COWDREY

Even though he was not the most charismatic of cricketers, Colin Cowdrey was undoubtedly one of the most elegant. So reliant did England become on his technique that, at the age of 42 and after three years out of Test cricket, he was flown to Australia to face Dennis Lillee and Jeff Thomson. Sometimes, his batting in his heyday was too introspective but his genius was obvious from an early age and immediately after leaving Oxford he made his Test debut against Australia amid rave reviews. He captained England 27 times between 1959 and 1969 and led his beloved Kent for 14 years. He made 1,000 runs in a season no less than 27 times overseas and 21 times in England and was knighted in 1992. Altogether he played in 114 Tests, averaging an impressive 44.06.

TRUEMAN THE INTIMIDATOR

The rivalry between Fred Trueman and the emergent Geoffrey Boycott at Yorkshire cricket club is legendary, but this story shows another side to the great bowler. Boycott explains: 'As a youngster on the fringe of the first team, I watched Fred scare the opposition. He was the best bowler I've seen at knocking over the last few batsman. When I got in the side, I would get into the dressing room early and Fred was never there. When I asked where he was, the old heads would smile and say go and look in the opposition dressing room. One day I did and Fred was holding court with their youngsters.

'Now lad, what number does thee bat?' asked Trueman.

'Number Four,' the youngster replied.

'Good,' said Trueman, 'that's two wickets I've got in this game.'

taking six wickets, despite a shoulder injury, as he held England to only 70 runs to defeat them at Old Trafford. Stirling Moss, having recovered from his injuries, won the 1961 Monaco Grand Prix and established his reputation as the greatest of his era, but crashed early in the 1962 season at Goodwood and retired. His departure was quickly papered over in British motor sport by the rise of other outstanding drivers such as Englishman Graham Hill who finished the year as the world drivers' champion ahead of Jim Clark of Scotland. Clark made amends the following year by becoming the youngest champion to date in Formula One history. Surtees, meanwhile, made his debut on four wheels with a Formula Junior Cooper for Ken Tyrrell and later drove a Lotus to second place at the British Grand Prix in only his second Formula One race. It was a good start...and by 1964, he was world champion.

But motor sport was, obviously, a very dangerous occupation. In June, 1960, at the

JIM CLARK – A TRUE RACING GREAT

World Formula One drivers' champion in 1963 and 1965, Jim Clark beat the record of the great Juan Manuel Fangio when he secured 25 race wins, including seven in one season. In all, Clark totalled 274 points from his 72 races. Son of a Scottish sheep farmer, he made his world championship debut for Lotus in 1960 and drove with them for the rest of his career. His first win was at Pau in 1961 and in addition to his two world titles, he was runner-up on three occasions. Killed at Hockenheim when his Formula Two Lotus left the track and hit a tree, he was a natural driver of enormous technical perfection and was sorely missed after his untimely death.

GEORGE BEST – A FLAWED GENIUS

If Tom Finney was the best player of the 1950s, then 'Georgie,' as all the girls called him, was surely the superstar of the 1960s. In an era of long hair, Carnaby Street and The Beatles, Best was the ultimate footballing sex symbol with a string of admirers constantly in tow and footballing skills to make fans of either sex drool in admiration. Best had the world at his feet. He won the first of his 31 caps for Northern Ireland before his 18th birthday and played a vital part in Manchester United's defeat of Benfica in 1968. Towards the end of his career, Best began to miss training sessions with worrying regularity and was dropped by club and country, as alcohol problems took hold. He was later recalled by both but the decline had set in and his brilliant but short-lived career was almost over, bar a spate of appearances for a number of low-key clubs at the end of his playing days.

Above: Mary Rand makes her world and Olympic record-breaking jump in Tokyo for which she won gold.

daunting Spa-Francorchamps circuit in Belgium, this was proved again when two British drivers, Chris Bristow, 22, and Alan Stacey, 26, were killed in the Belgian Grand Prix. Their deaths followed serious accidents the previous day involving Stirling Moss, then 30, and Michael Taylor, 25. Stacey's death was reported to be due to a freak accident when a bird flew into his face and smashed his goggles. He was driving at a place known as the 'fountain of the bird', according to WA McKenzie's report in *The Daily Telegraph*, when it happened. He lost control of his Lotus, at 140 mph, and it hit a bank and burst into flames. Bristow's Cooper car somersaulted three times when he lost control of it at 130 mph on the fast Burneville corner.

Above: Ann Packer receives her gold medal for winning the women's 800 metres at the 1964 Tokyo Olympics.

SHORT-SIGHTED SUCCESS

The image of Bobby Charlton, his unrivalled midfield class and the clutch of goals he scored with blistering shots from outside the area, were one of the enduring sporting memories from the sixties and seventies. However, according to his brother Jack, it could have been so very different. Jack recalls: 'Bobby only became a world class midfield player by accident. That accident was Nobby Stiles. When Nobby got into the first team at United, and then for England, he would win the ball and Bobby had to stay within 15 yards of him, because that is as far as Nobby could see!'

By the 1960s, the World Cup was a regular and respected global event and, in 1962, England travelled to Chile for the tournament. During the event, they beat Argentina with a fluent display but were knocked out in the quarter-finals by Brazil, the eventual winners, who defended their trophy successfully. Once again, Pele played a prominent part in Brazil's success, but the top goalscorer was Edvaldo Izidio Neto, better known as Vava. Other big names in action that summer were Sonny Liston and Floyd Patterson, the former knocking out the latter in

MATT BUSBY – THE MAN WITH THE MIDAS TOUCH

It is hard to find enough superlatives to describe the influence that one man can have had on one club. Matt Busby, later knighted, was not the most popular of managers with all his players but he will forever be known as the man who survived the Munich air disaster and went on to mastermind Manchester United's European Cup triumph of 1968. He only ever won one international cap for Scotland, at a time when, ironically, he was playing club football for Manchester City. Indeed, he had a somewhat moderate playing career but all that changed when he went into management.
In all he guided Manchester United for 25 years, winning not only the European Cup against Benfica at Wembley but also the league championship five times and the FA Cup twice. Busby himself was close to death after the Munich air crash but survived from the wreckage of the so-called 'Busby Babes' to build another, equally strong squad that has only recently been matched in quality by Alex Ferguson's team.

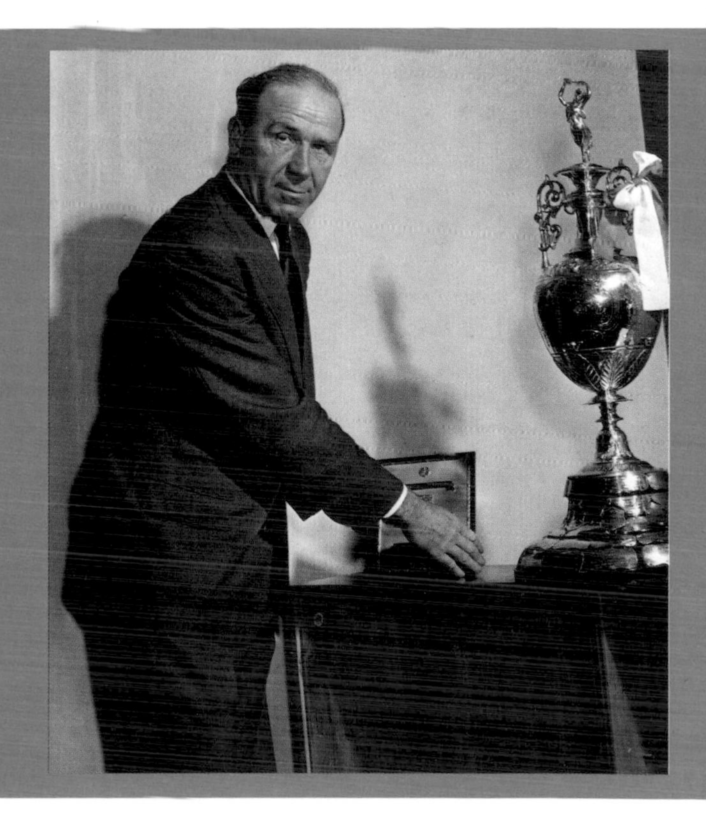

BASIL D'OLIVEIRA AND APARTHEID

Basil d'Oliveira became more significant than he could ever have imagined when, in 1966, he walked on to the field to play for England at Lord's. By doing so, he gave new hope to a generation of under-privileged coloured people in South Africa, his native homeland. In those days the apartheid system was still very much in place and the idea of a coloured player who was brought up in South Africa playing against them for another country was something the South Africans could not contemplate.

When England's team to play South Africa was announced in 1968, d'Oliveira's name was not on it despite the fact that, in the previous series against Australia, he had scored 158 in the victorious fifth and final Test. His omission, clearly for political reasons, drew protests from MPs and a special meeting was called by the MCC to protest that d'Oliveira should be included after all. When Tom Cartwright was reported injured, it gave the selectors the perfect opportunity to bring d'Oliveira back in. At which point the South Africans refused to allow d'Oliveira entry and the tour was cancelled. England did not play South Africa again until the end of apartheid.

Above: Alf Ramsey with the Jules Rimet trophy in August 1966. It remains the only World Cup that any British football team has ever won.

just two minutes and six seconds to take the world heavyweight boxing championship.

In June, 1963, Henry Cooper fought Cassius Clay, later to be known as Muhammad Ali, but previously described as the Louisville Lip, at Wembley. Cooper's famous left hook landed once and floored the big-talking showman who had predicted he would win in five rounds; but it was not enough. Clay did indeed win in five with blood spurting from the cuts around Cooper's left eye.

Alf Ramsey became England manager this year, too, and Spurs, on Wednesday, May 15, beat Atletico Madrid to win the European Cup

THE BOYS OF '66

When Kenneth Wolstenholme uttered the immortal words 'They think it's all over.... it is now,' to millions of television viewers in the dying moments of the 1966 World Cup final, it heralded scenes of jubilation never witnessed before or since in the country that invented the game. To the disappointment of a succession of subsequent managers, no one has been able to emulate the success of Alf Ramsey and the red-shirted team that was led by the late Bobby Moore and included the likes of the Charlton brothers, Bobby and Jack, goalkeeper Gordon Banks and tireless workers like Nobby Stiles and Alan Ball.

Banks, Moore and Bobby Charlton were the backbone of the side that was dubbed the 'wingless wonders' by the media for playing a system that had no place for out-and-out wingers. It also, controversially, had no place for Jimmy Greaves. Yet so strong was Ramsey's self-belief that he risked the nation's wrath by leaving Greaves out of the final, opting instead for Geoff Hurst.

The rest, as they say, is history, with Hurst scoring a unique hat-trick that finally defeated a German side that never gave up and forced extra time in the dying seconds of the regulation 90 minutes. Ramsey, in his bright blue tracksuit, marched on to the field and told the England team that they had effectively won the World Cup once, now they had to do it again. 'Look at them,' said Ramsey, pointing to the Germans sprawled out on the grass. 'They're finished.' What happened next is one of the all-time great moments of British sport. Hurst's second and England's third goal is still one of the most talked-about strikes in the history of world football. His shot hit the underside of the bar, bounced down and then out and away. The Russian linesman raised his flag to signal a goal, the Germans protested vehemently but the referee agreed.

The Germans, as they had done after going 2-1 down during normal time, threw their men into attack in search of yet another equaliser. But their defence broke down. Moore, who had a wonderful match, sent Hurst through with what Jack Charlton many years later described as 'the best pass that I have ever seen to a running player.' Hurst beat the German keeper with a blistering shot to make the score 4-2 and win the cup.

Winners' Cup. It was some compensation for missing out the previous year on glory when they were defeated by Benfica in the semi-finals of the European Cup, 4-3 on aggregate. Limited overs cricket arrived with the launch of the Gillette Cup in which Sussex beat Worcestershire.

In 1964, two Englishmen broke cricketing records. Fred Trueman became the first bowler to take 300 Test wickets when Colin Cowdrey caught Neil Hawke off his delivery in a match against Australia and Ken Barrington became the first man to score centuries against all seven Test-playing countries when he performed the

WAS IT OVER THE LINE?

Sir Bobby Charlton and his old adversary Franz Beckenbauer are great friends, but one debate still rumbles on between them. 'Every time I meet Franz,' says Bobby, 'he goes on about that dreaded third goal in the World Cup final in which he claims the ball didn't go over the line. I got so fed up that I suggested the next time we met we would watch the whole game and then put the matter to bed. So we did. We sat together and watched the game and the extra time. At the end Franz said to me: "You were right, England were the better team, you wanted it more."
"Good," I said. "No more about it." Then, I met him three months later and he said: "Bobby, about that third goal..."'

GARETH EDWARDS – LEADING WALES TO SUCCESS

After winning his first cap for Wales as a 19-year-old against France in 1967, the Cardiff scrum-half never missed a match for his country. Born in Swansea in 1947, he made 53 consecutive international appearances — 13 as captain — and won his final cap in 1978. During his career, Wales enjoyed a glorious spell of success, notching up seven championships, five triple crowns and two Grand Slams. His jinking runs and memorable half-back partnerships with Barry John and Phil Bennett contributed enormously to this success. Edwards also took part in three British Lions tours including the visit to New Zealand where the Lions won their first series victory against the All Blacks.

feat against South Africa. In the Tokyo Olympics, Mary Rand, with a record jump, and Lynn Davies won the respective women's and men's long jump gold medals, while Ann Packer won silver in the 400 metres and then gold in the 800 metres.

In football, dark shadows. Two Sheffield Wednesday players, Peter Swan and David Layne, and a former player, Tony Kay, were reportedly involved in bribery allegations surrounding a fixture against Ipswich. Elsewhere, Cassius Clay, as an underdog, beat Sonny Liston

Above: Clive Rowlands, scrum-half and captain, led Wales to two Five Nations championships in the early 1960s.

by a knockout in the seventh round to win the world heavyweight title at Miami Beach.

The next year, back to football, and Leeds did everything but emulate Spurs' double achievement. Only ill-fortune stopped them. Beaten in the struggle for the league championship by Manchester United on goal difference, they lost the FA Cup final to Liverpool. So near, yet so far, for a team that was often to be regarded as the bridesmaids of the English game. The same year, Jock Stein took over at Celtic just in time to sit back and, in 1966, watch England win the World Cup with a team built from the backbone of the West Ham side which won the European Cup Winners' Cup on May 20, 1965, by beating Munich 1860 2-0.

The summer of 1966 was something special. Not only did England win the Jules Rimet trophy, but Jonah Barrington became world number one at squash and Derek Underwood, aged only 21, made his debut for England's cricket team as a left-arm spinner. But the World Cup win overshadowed everything, delivering, as Alf Ramsey had promised, a great triumph for the England team in which Gordon Banks, Bobby Moore, Bobby Charlton and Geoff Hurst performed with high class.

In 1967, Gareth Edwards made his debut for Wales' rugby team, aged 19. But the bigger celebrations were for Glasgow Celtic, under Stein's guidance, as they became the first British team to win the European Cup, defeating Inter Milan 2-1 in Lisbon. Many of their fans, it was reported, stayed in Portugal and settled into a new life. But it was a sad summer for British cyclist Tommy Simpson, whose great effort in the Tour de France ended when he died of heat exhaustion.

A year later, in 1968, while students were rioting in Paris and around Europe, there were political uprisings of a different kind in cricket. England's Basil d'Oliveira was told he was unwelcome in South Africa, where England were set to tour and so the MCC cancelled their plans. Colin Cowdrey, in an entirely non-political act, became the first player to appear in 100 Test matches and Arthur Ashe, a charming American much loved by the public, became the first black player to win a major tennis title when he won the US Open. He also won the men's singles at Wimbledon seven years later. Big events, all of them: but none

Above: Bobby Charlton (right) and Shay Brennan celebrate Manchester United's European Cup triumph over Benfica in 1968.

reverberated in Britain for as long or as loud as Manchester United's long-awaited European Cup triumph, a 4-1 victory over Benfica, after extra time, at Wembley.

What a night! What a team! Denis Law lay in a hospital bed, recovering from injury and surrounded by nurses, as his team, the team built by Matt Busby from the wreckage of Munich, finally delivered the trophy that their Scottish manager had pursued so passionately and for so long. It was a magical evening, a warm, hazy night. John Aston, an unsung squad member and a left winger of pace, enjoyed the match of his life. Bobby Charlton scored twice. Brian Kidd, just 19, scored once. And George Best, arguably the greatest footballer of all time, certainly the greatest British player of all time, danced through to

Above: Tony Jacklin holds the Claret Jug after winning the 1969 Open championship at Royal Lytham.

'ENRY'S HAMMER

Henry Cooper was British, Commonwealth and European heavyweight boxing champion, so it was natural that he should get a shot at the world title. So it was at Wembley Stadium in 1963 that the Londoner took on the then Cassius Clay, soon to be Muhammed Ali. Famously Cooper caught Clay with a left hook that could, and perhaps should, have put him out for the count. But Clay recovered, Cooper was cut — a career-long problem — and Ali went on to become the greatest fighter of all time. 'Ali paid me the greatest compliment when he said my punch not only shook him but shook his ancestors back in Africa,' recalled Cooper, who firmly established himself as one of England's sporting legends during his career.

BILL SHANKLY

Of all the quotations attributed to British managers, none has stood the test of time longer than Bill Shankly's immortal line: 'Football is not a matter of life and death: it's far more important. 'The man behind the rise of Liverpool after joining in December 1959, he led the Anfield side to unprecedented success during a golden era in the club's history which saw them dominate on both the home and European fronts.

He harboured an almost fanatical desire to win which was also carried on to the training field. Liverpool legend Tommy Smith recalled what it was like playing for Shanks. 'In the year that I signed for Liverpool, the apprentices would work on the ground throughout the summer. We trained on the car park at Anfield, and as we had no opposition the local bin men would come along once a week, and we would play 14-a-side. Bill would not allow the game to finish until we won. 1-0 or 12-11 did not matter, as long as we won.

LOOK BEFORE YOU TACKLE

Nobby Stiles' first international call-up was for the under-23s, in Aberdeen against Scotland. Nobby, who has incredibly poor eyesight, had forgotten his contact lenses for the game, but refused to tell Alf Ramsey. Scotland and, in particular, Charlie Cooke dominated the first half of the game which was played in dreadful, snowy conditions with poor visibility. At half-time Ramsey told Nobby to sort Cooke out. Nobby was more than happy to oblige. 'My chance came early in the second half,' he recalled, 'the ball bounced and I hit Charlie Cooke with a storming challenge. Not dirty but hard and he went down in a heap. Then Norman Hunter came over and asked me what I had done.

"I've clattered Charlie, that's what I've done,"

"Have another look," he replied.

It wasn't Cooke, but former Leeds hardman, Billy Bremner.

"You b******,' said Bremner. "I'll get you for this, Stiles."'

But he never did and the two remained great friends.

crown his and his club's season. It echoed all that was best, too, from the 1966 World Cup finals when Eusebio's Portugal had been defeated by Bobby Charlton's England. This time, the two met again in their club shirts and the same man and his English team won.

It was perhaps the glory of that May night which inspired Leeds even more the following season. For, in the spring of 1969, Don Revie's often-dour, sometimes-delightful, but always competitive Leeds United won their first league championship title with a massive 67 points. Manchester United had begun to fall into decline. Tony Jacklin won the British Open golf championship, and Great Britain & Ireland shared the Ryder Cup with the United States at Royal Birkdale after Jack Nicklaus conceded a putt to Jacklin at the final hole.

1970-1979

WINNING AT ALL COSTS

8

AFTER A DECADE LIKE THE SIXTIES, filled with joy and triumph, it was always going to be difficult for British sport to maintain such special charmed momentum. There is no doubt the 1970s were years of equally great British sporting feats — from the championships of Jackie Stewart in Formula One to Liverpool's dominance of European football, from Tony Jacklin's success in the United States Open golf championship to Ian Botham's emergence as one of cricket's finest all-rounders and greatest characters, from David Bedford's phenomenal 10,000 metres running to David Wilkie's swimming in the Olympics 200 metres breaststroke. But the enchanting mixture of pop and sport, old charm and modern media, amateur ethics and progressive methods which made the 1960s a unique decade for many reasons was replaced by an altogether different atmosphere. If anything, the 1970s ushered in the era of 'money-money-money' and the rise of a win-at-all-costs attitude, which separated sport from dignity.

Botham was an arresting, turbulent — sometimes truculent — but fascinating and often abrasive embodiment of this age, rising from an ordinary background to break down the old social barriers of Test cricket with an all-action and outspoken style carried on in other sports by such rising stars as Nigel Mansell in motor racing, Charlie George in football, Alex Higgins in snooker, Barry Sheene in motor cycling and, later still, by Paul Gascoigne.

Sport rose beyond its previous boundaries in every way and began to command more and more attention, thereby becoming not only a recreational occupation of increasingly high standards, but a vehicle for media stardom, a means of getting rich quick and gaining worldly successes which attracted the eye of the

Right: Virginia Wade wins the Wimbledon ladies' singles title in 1977, the championship's centenary year.

RED RUM RUNS INTO LEGEND

It is unlikely that there will ever be a steeplechaser quite so legendary as the horse who became known to a nation as 'Rummie'. Red Rum's success was the stuff of fantasy as he won the Grand National an incredible three times in the 1970s. His first victory, in 1973, transformed what seemed a certain victory for Crisp into what was the fastest National ever run. The following year, carrying 12 stone, the race lifted him into the immortals when he became the first back-to-back National winner for 38 years.

The following two years saw L'Escargot and Rag Trade win the race but in 1977 Rummie achieved what no horse had ever done in 140 years — win a third National. When he retired a life-size bronze statue was erected in 1988 at Aintree to celebrate his unique achievements.

Perhaps the greatest irony is that Red Rum was the ultimate underdog. He achieved everything against the odds after originally being rejected as a flat horse before becoming a legend in the hands of 'Ginger' McCain, a former taxi driver and used car salesman.

FRANCIS SIGNS
FOR FOREST
FOR 1 MILLION POUNDS.

GORDON BANKS AND THAT SAVE

Who will ever forget the sight of England's legendary goalkeeper leaping instinctively to keep out a Pele header that seemed certain to end up in the net in the 1970 World Cup? Such was the quality of Banks' one-handed piece of acrobatic brilliance in Mexico that it has become the one save to which other great stops are regularly compared.

As well as helping England to the World Cup in 1966, Banks also won Football League Cup winners' medals for Leicester in 1964 and Stoke in 1972, his outstanding performance in the latter doing much to earn him the award as Footballer of the Year. It was the same year, sadly, that Banks' career virtually ended after an horrendous car accident cost him the sight of one eye. Later he fought and won a battle against a life-threatening stomach tumour. 'In my career I broke fingers, ribs, my collarbone and had knee injuries,' said Banks. 'I lost an eye, had stomach problems yet when I am at dinner parties, some people still come up to me and ask if I am still playing.'

Above: Barry Sheene at Silverstone in practice for the 1977 John Player Grand Prix.

financial and political worlds and which created commercial opportunities. These, in turn, helped turn sportsmen and sportswomen into role models in a way that fundamentally changed British sport and, at the same time, encouraged some stars to challenge the establishment. Anyone could succeed and everyone wanted to try.

If the stars of earlier decades had risen from poor backgrounds and enjoyed success, it had been in a modest manner and without the same opportunities for making themselves wealthy inside and outside their sports. Sponsorship and television combined to ignite an explosion which saw British sport change beyond recognition from the almost-dreamy days of Corinthian values and simple objectives which had preceded the 1960s. No more flannels and blazers. This was the age of denims and sport was in the spotlight.

This evolution was clearly manifested in a few examples of events and personalities of the

JAMES HUNT – THE PLAYBOY RACER

James Hunt brought fun and flair to the Grand Prix arena as his captivating persona caused women to swoon with one glance at his disarming smile and his rivals to look on with envy at his driving talent. As much at home enjoying the glamourous trappings associated with Formula One, the party-loving Hunt made no secret of his love for the fast life off track, but his natural prowess behind the steering wheel won him many admirers.

Following his development in the British Formula Three championship, Hunt graduated into Grand Prix racing in 1973 where he proved himself courtesy of a famous driving duel against rival Niki Lauda. Driving at the Dutch Zandvoort circuit in 1975, Hunt out-raced the Ferrari of Lauda to claim his first victory. It was the start of a dramatic rise which saw him switch from Hesketh to the McLaren team to replace Emerson Fittipaldi the following season.

He duly repaid the faith of McLaren by again beating Lauda. This time it was to claim the 1976 world drivers' crown which he won with just a one point advantage. A year in which Hunt tasted victory at the Nurburgring, Zandvoort, Mosport Park and Watkins Glen, he was the embodiment of the classically cool racing driver.

Above: The Arsenal double-winning side of 1970-71. Their achievements equalled those of their North London rivals, Tottenham Hotspur, who won the League and Cup double 10 years earlier.

Left: Willie John McBride led the British Lions to unprecedented success during their 1974 tour to South Africa.

Below: After winning a thrilling battle for the 1969 world championship, Jackie Stewart continued to maintain the high standards of British motor racing drivers throughout the 1970s.

1970s. The worst was the tragedy at the 1972 Olympics in Munich where, on September 5, a gang of 'black September' Arab guerrillas broke into the Israeli quarters in the Olympic village. Eleven Israeli Olympic hostages were to die in the siege that became a bloodbath after an attempted rescue by the German police ended in disaster. It was an episode which tarnished not only the Olympic movement's reputation, but that of international sport by demonstrating how a high-profile sports event can be hijacked for the worst possible political ends.

Other images of the seventies that help conjure up a decade of dazzling achievements, decadence and delirium came from Muhammad Ali reaching the peak of his remarkable boxing career, the elegant David Gower batting as if born to it, Willie John McBride's success with the conquering British Lions rugby team, the

MOORE AND PELE – TWO GREATS COLLIDE

Great sporting icons are few and far between. Two heroes playing each other at their peak is rarer still, but the battle between the world's greatest footballer Pele, and the master of defending, Bobby Moore, was undoubtedly one such occasion. The high-profile setting for their clash in the 1970 World Cup proved an adequate stage as both players distinguished themselves in a tightly-fought game. Pele's Brazil won 1-0.

Pele set up team-mate Jairzinho for the goal, while Moore's high-level display included a tackle of such importance and precise timing in the England area when he stopped Jairzinho in his tracks, that it left onlookers shaking their heads in disbelief. After the match the pair traded shirts, smiles and hugged, in scenes that set the standard for sporting endeavour.

Right: Robin Cousins (pictured) and John Curry helped raise the public profile of ice skating throughout the 1970s. Their success was continued, in ice dance, by Torvill and Dean in the 1980s.

captivating gymnastics of Olga Korbut and Nadia Comaneci, Pele's inspirational leadership of the 1970 World Cup winners Brazil, Arsenal's double of 1971, the calypso cricket of the West Indies and Bjorn Borg's dominance of Wimbledon.

There was some room, still, for the understated and self-effacing humourists who had always lived in the changing rooms of British sport, the individuals and mavericks, but their days were numbered. Methodologists and managers were moving in, success was soon to be everything and sport as big business and global industry was on the way.

Jackie Stewart, an icon of the sixties with his long hair and easy grin, had signed off the old decade with a thrilling triumph in the 1969 drivers' world championship by winning a wheel-to-wheel battle at Monza with Jochen Rindt in a close-fought race that involved five drivers. He succeeded the dry-witted and debonair Graham Hill as title-holder and he continued his successes into the early 1970s which opened with Tony Jacklin winning the US Open golf championship by seven strokes.

The first year of the new decade was momentous. Brazil won the World Cup in Mexico, defeating Italy 4-1 in a magnificent and memorable final, inspired by Pele. It was their third triumph in the competition and they retained the Jules Rimet trophy outright. On

the way to the final, the Brazilians overcame England in a superb early group game. England were knocked out in the quarter-finals when they lost 3-2 to West Germany after leading 2-0 before manager Alf Ramsey substituted Bobby Charlton, a decision which allowed Franz Beckenbauer to take control.

Margaret Court won Wimbledon, but, sadly, while Muhammad Ali returned to boxing after a three-year absence, Sonny Liston died from a drugs overdose and Rindt — Stewart's challenger of 1969 in Italy — was killed in a crash back at Monza in the 1970 Italian Grand Prix. When the season finished, however, he was declared world champion posthumously. In athletics, the sport mourned the loss on Boxing Day, 1970, of one of its most illustrious and popular stars, Lillian Board, aged 22, who died from cancer. She was the Olympic silver medallist at the 400 metres in 1968 when she was also declared the BBC's Sportswoman of the Year.

In tennis, Great Britain, with David Lloyd missing, experienced their worst Davis Cup defeat when they lost 3-2 to Austria in the first round of a European zone competition, but in football, Manchester City added the European Cup Winners' Cup to their success in the League Cup, beating Gornik Zabrze 2-1, Neil Young and Francis Lee scoring City's goals. A cricket tour of England by South Africa was cancelled eight days before it was due to start, amid threats by 12 African nation members of the British Commonwealth not to take part in the 1970 Commonwealth Games in Edinburgh.

In 1971, India, with Bishan Bedi and Co, came to England and won a Test match for the first time. It was a first signal that a new order in world cricket was on the way. In golf, Lee Trevino followed Jacklin by winning the US and British Open titles while in horse racing Mill

VIRGINIA WADE PROVIDES CENTENARY CELEBRATION CHEER

Timing is eveything in sport, and Virginia Wade could not have picked a better occasion to win her first, and only, Wimbledon ladies' singles title than in 1977 at the Centennial celebrations of one of British sport's largest and most traditional events. In her 16th championships, when many believed her chance of claiming the title had passed, Wade proved otherwise. She defeated Dutch player Betty Stove on a packed Centre Court in front of the Queen, 4-6, 6-3, 6-1. Prior to her success at Wimbledon, Wade's previous singles titles came in the 1968 US Open and 1972 Australian Open.

Born in Hampshire, Wade was raised in South Africa until she returned to England at 15 before taking a science degree at Sussex University. Tennis was her calling though, and after an illustrious career which included a record 100 Federation Cup matches for Britain and 20 Wightman Cup ties, she became the first woman to be elected to the Wimbledon Championships Committee.

FIGHTING BACK

Gordon Brown, the famous Scottish second row, was a member of the 1974 British Lions squad that swept all before them, and recalled one instance which served notice to South Africa of the visitors' and Willie John McBride's intentions. Brown recalled that during one game the brutality of the South Africans had become unacceptable. McBride told the referee that he should sort out the roughnecks or, he warned, 'We will.'

The referee ignored the request so McBride called his forwards around him. 'When I call 99 you hit the nearest one to you,' he said. Brown was aghast. But in the next scrum the ball was heeled to Gareth Edwards and, as the skipper called the magic number, all hell broke lose. The resultant punch-up sorted out the Springboks, and most of the trouble, before the Lions pack went on to dominate the rest of the tour.

Reef won the Derby, the King George VI and the Prix de l'Arc de Triomphe. Football suffered mixed fortunes in 1971 with an Arsenal league and cup double, inspired by Frank McLintock, and earlier, in January, with the worst spectator tragedy in Britain, at Ibrox Stadium, when 66 people died at the end of the Rangers v Celtic clash. The tragedy came at the Copland Road end of the ground when a large number of people, who were leaving the stadium after seeing Celtic score first after 88 minutes, surged back on hearing news that Rangers had equalised. Witnesses said that the result was a massive human surge and the collapse of steep steps behind the terracing. 'The crowd fell like a pack of cards,' said one.

The following year, cricket was changing route and the one-day game became established when Dennis Amiss hit the first century in one-

Above: Liverpool manager Bill Shankly (right) and his future successor Bob Paisley. Liverpool were the dominant force in English football throughout the 1970s and 1980s.

Opposite: Mary Peters leaps to victory in the 1972 Olympic Games. She took gold in the pentathlon.

Below: Osvaldo Ardiles and Ricardo Villa meet their new Spurs fans. The Argentine pair were the first foreign players to join English football; by the late 1990s the foreign influx had reached incredible proportions.

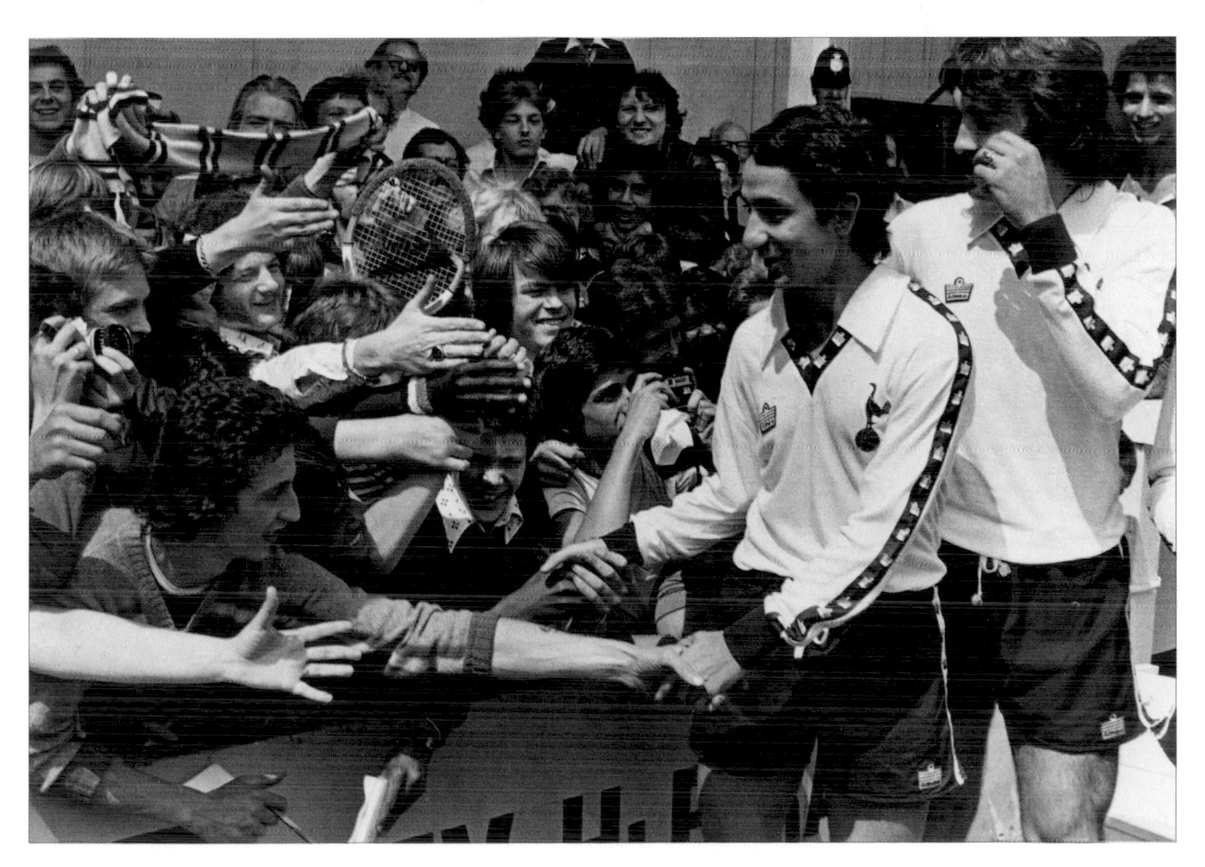

day cricket as England beat Australia 2-1 to win the first Prudential Trophy. At least they were still playing in whites. In the same year, Alex Higgins won the snooker world championship, Mark Spitz won seven swimming gold medals at the Olympics where his feats were over-shadowed by tragedy, and Giacomo Agostino won the 500cc motorcycling world title for the seventh consecutive year.

In 1973, the Charlton brothers, Jack and Bobby, retired from football, a bomb scare interrupted play at Lord's during England's Test match against the West Indies and David Bedford — he of the famous trademark 'bandito' moustache — sliced eight seconds off Lasse Viren's record in the 10,000 metres. Formula One driver Mike Hailwood earned a George Medal for displaying honourable courage when rescuing an unconscious Gianclaudio Regazzoni by pulling him away from his flaming car at the South African Grand Prix. In boxing, George Foreman (still around at the end of the century) knocked down Joe Frazier six times in two rounds as he took the world heavyweight championship. Wimbledon's tennis tournament remained synonymous with something more poetic throughout these times, retaining grass courts and white kit, and in 1974 it enjoyed some romance as the champions Jimmy Connors and Chris Evert became engaged and won the men's and ladies' singles. The image endured, but the romance did not.

In 1975, English football saw the first of that late 20th century phenomenon also known as Wimbledon, aka The Dons. As a Southern League football team, they rose and scrapped with intense ferocity, beating First Division Burnley in an FA Cup tie and then drawing with mighty Leeds United. It was the year, too, when one of the south London borough's most famous

ALEX HIGGINS – THE WILDMAN OF SNOOKER

One of the most naturally gifted players ever to grace a snooker table, the flamboyant and mercurial Alex 'Hurricane' Higgins thrust himself into the hearts of fans and record books when he won the coveted world title at his first attempt in 1972. He was 23 at the time and became the youngest player to win the world championships. His uniquely fast and all-action style set a precedent in the game, which helped snooker rise to a new degree of popularity.

A fiery personality with little regard for the establishment, he had several run-ins with the snooker hierarchy but Higgins was a firm favourite with fans, enthralling the crowds as he won the 1980 British Gold Cup, 1983 UK Open and Benson and Hedges Masters tournaments of 1978 and 1981.

His second world championship arrived 10 years after his first, when he defeated six-times winner Ray Reardon. Higgins, hugging his wife and young baby in celebration, could not hold back the tears.

WILLIE JOHN McBRIDE AND HIS BRITISH LIONS HEROES

In an era when the power and presence of southern hemisphere rugby dominated the international rugby union scene, Willie John McBride, captain of the British Lions, rose successfully to topple the Springboks during a memorable 1974 Lions tour. It was the fifth Lions tour and turned out to be the most successful ever after they returned to Britain undefeated in 22 games, winning all but one, and stunning the South Africans in the Test series.

Aiming for a clean sweep of victories at Ellis Park in front of 75,000 spectators, Fergus Slattery thought the Lions had claimed a last-gasp victory after he crashed over the Springboks line. Referee Max Baise, however, had already blown for a five yard scrum. Nevertheless, that could not take the gloss off the way McBride led his team on the field and inspired his team-mates to even greater heights than they had imagined.

McBride's international career lasted from 1962 to 1975 during which time he played a record 17 Tests for the Lions and 63 Tests, of which 12 were as captain, for Ireland. A colossus of a figure, he and his team returned to a heroes' welcome after a tour in which they won 21, drew one, and lost none.

Above: Ray Reardon won the world snooker championship six times during his career, but incredibly that feat was bettered by the Scot, Stephen Hendry, in 1999.

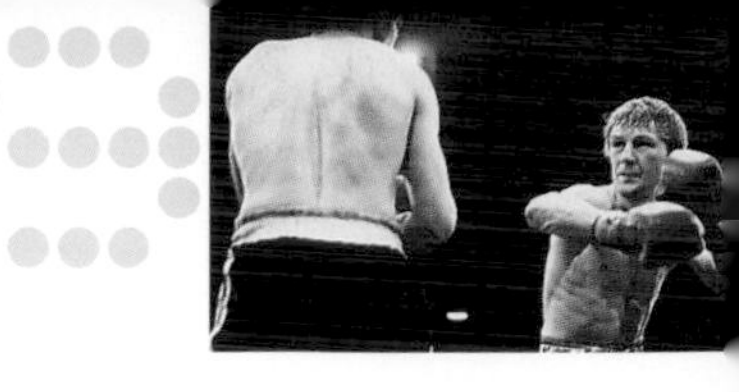

Above: In 1977 Geoff Boycott, batting here for Yorkshire, scored his 100th century in first-class cricket.

Opposite: The late 1970s witnessed the emergence of Ian Botham onto the cricketing scene. He would become one of the game's finest all-rounders.

future tennis champions, Czechoslovakia's Martina Navratilova defected to the United States; Niki Lauda won the Formula One world drivers' title for Ferrari; and Ali beat Frazier in the 15th round of the 'Thrilla in Manila.'

The following year, 1976, saw another southern team cause an FA Cup upset, but this time it was Southampton, of the Second Division, who beat Manchester United in the final at Wembley, thanks to a goal from Bobby Stokes, while James Hunt claimed the Formula One drivers' crown by one point from Niki Lauda. David Wilkie won the 200 metres breaststroke at the Olympics and England's cricketers ran into difficulties against ferocious fast bowling from both the West Indies and Australia.

In a Test match at The Oval, Michael Holding took 14 wickets for 149, as his team

SHOW THEM WHO'S BOSS

The talents of Bill Shankly, master tactician and king of the Liverpool empire in the 1970s, didn't stretch to a knowledge of women. Denis Law recalled Shankly giving him a talking-to on the opposite sex during his time at Anfield as a 15-year-old apprentice. 'Bill called all the apprentices together one day' recalled Law, 'and told us that if we were thinking of getting married, to always show the woman who was the boss. He said: "Do as I did to Nessie (Mrs Shankly). On our wedding night on the way to our honeymoon, I took her to watch Rochdale reserves." '

OLD FIRM CLASH AT IBROX HIT BY TRAGEDY AS 66 DIE

On January 2, 1971, 66 people died and more than 200 were injured following a game between Old Firm rivals Rangers and Celtic. About 80,000 fans turned up to watch the game, but many had begun to depart just prior to the final whistle as Celtic led 1-0. On their way out, however, a roar arose from the home crowd following Colin Stein's late equaliser, and as fans streamed back into the ground, disaster struck. Clashing with supporters still trying to make their way out, the strain was too much for staircase 13 to handle and, even though the stadium had been built to cater for large crowds, crush barriers buckled. This resulted in fans falling down the long staircase and as the effect dominoed, the tragic loss of life could not be prevented.

Above: Kevin Keegan was a prolific goalscorer for both club and country and led from the front as captain of England.

crushed the English by 231 runs while, the following year, in the Centenary Test, Dennis Lillee took 11 wickets to seal an Australian victory. Falling short of the 463 England had been set to win, despite a innings of 174 by Derek Randall, the winning margin was 45 runs, which amazingly was the same as in the inaugural Test match. Geoffrey Boycott scored his 100th hundred but it was time for a new generation of English cricketers and they were led by Botham, who later that year took five for 74 against Australia at Nottingham when he made his Test debut, and Gower when he arrived soon after.

In 1977, however, others were to take the headlines in British sport as the Queen celebrated her silver jubilee year. Red Rum, arguably the most famous and popular horse of all time, won a third Grand National and retired; Kevin Keegan played his last game for Liverpool as they lifted the European Cup; and Virginia Wade, finally, won the ladies' singles title at Wimbledon. If this was a fillip, in a valedictory sense, with so many glorious

departures, 1978 was even more encouraging as it brought in the new faces who were to carry sport on to even higher standards of expectation. Gower, for example, made his English Test cricket debut and struck a four with his first ball, Navratilova won at Wimbledon and Bernard Hinault won his first of a record five Tour de France titles.

Liverpool claimed the European Cup for the second successive year courtesy of a Kenny Dalglish goal in the 1-0 win against FC Bruges and Viv Anderson became the first black player to represent England in a full international, the Nottingham Forest full-back winning his first cap in-front of a home Wembley crowd in the 1-0 victory against Czechoslovakia.

By 1979, in football, it was clear that money was talking and transfer fees were escalating, but the first £1 million fee, paid by Nottingham Forest to Birmingham City for Trevor Francis, still came as a shock. That it was done by the sagacious old Forest manager Brian Clough was less of a surprise. It was a year of statistical achievements and landmarks: Ian Botham captured his 100th Test wicket in record time only two years and nine days after his debut; Sebastian Coe set world records in the 800 metres, 1500 metres and mile events; Jim Watt won the lightweight world championship boxing title; Maurice Hope took the light-middleweight crown; Severiano Ballesteros played from a car park on his way to victory in the British Open; and in the Ryder Cup, the first European team (after the extension from GB&I) was defeated by the United States.

Below: Jim Watt (right) was one of the finest fighters Scotland has produced. He capped an excellent career by winning the world lightweight title in 1979.

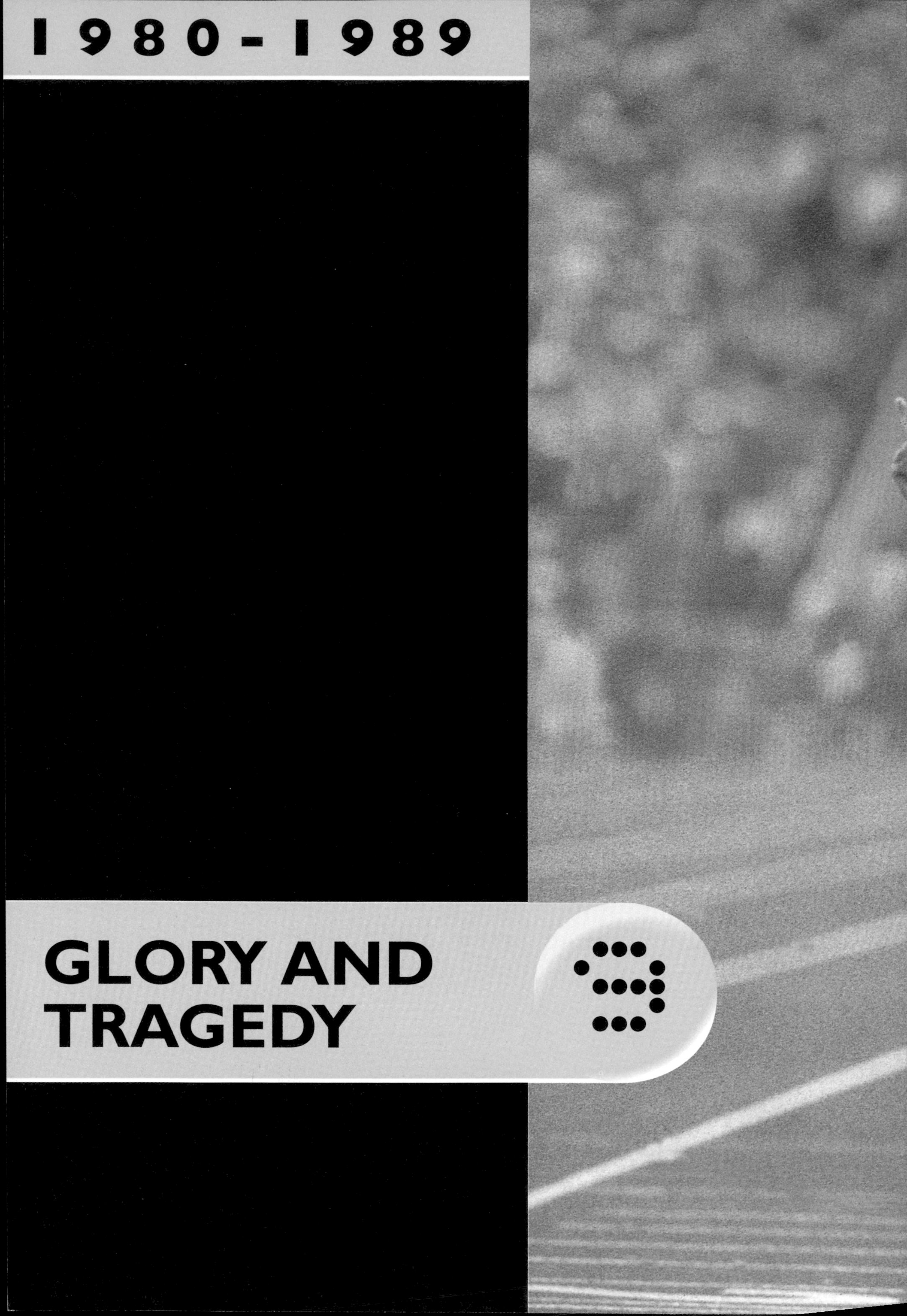
1980-1989
GLORY AND TRAGEDY
9

LA84
359

AND SO TO THE 1980s with sport booming everywhere, a new generation of stars rising rapidly, standards improving just as quickly and the competitive edge in everything encouraging younger and younger talents to rise beyond experienced men and reach the top. Great crowds, great rewards and, sadly, great tragedies: Bradford, Heysel and Hillsborough all illustrating that terrible dangers remained in a rapidly-advancing technological age.

The deaths of 40 people, rising to 52, in a blazing wooden grandstand, at the Bradford City v Lincoln City Third Division match; 41 people in Brussels, at the Liverpool v Juventus European Cup final of 1985; and 96 in Sheffield, when Liverpool played Nottingham Forest in an FA Cup semi-final, were a deep shock in a decade filled with dazzling achievements. They brought home, also, the truth that despite all the hyperbole that surrounded sport in modern television and radio commentaries, it was not a matter of life or death. This was. And the grief of the families of those who perished ensured that lessons were learned in such a profound fashion that British football, in particular, has since been entirely rebuilt.

But it was a marvellous decade of extremes for sport in so many other ways, heralding the arrival of the first London Marathon in 1981, the boom years for snooker and the great spectacles of the 1988 Seoul Olympics and the games of 1980 in Moscow where England's distance runners took the limelight.

Just listing the names brings back the buzz: Kenny Dalglish and Ian Rush (Liverpool's deadly striking duo), Jayne Torvill and Christopher Dean (golden successes in ice-dancing), Ian Botham (bat and ball), Nick Faldo (golf's workaholic champion), Adrian Moorhouse (record-breaking swimming in the 100 metres

Below: The first London Marathon in 1981 attracted a huge entry, which has grown steadily since.

DALEY THOMPSON – A SUPREME ALL-ROUNDER

Arrogant, brash, offensive. These were just three of the adjectives that were thrown at Daley Thompson during his remarkable career as the world's best decathlete. Love him or loathe him, no one could deny his genius in becoming the greatest all-round athlete the world has ever seen. Season after season Thompson would be written off, but he invariably defied the odds.

Born in north London, the son of a Nigerian father and Scottish mother, he won gold medals at both the 1980 and 1984 Olympics. In all Daley won 19 decathlons in major championships but curiously never contested a single tournament in England. Having rewritten all the record books, he tried for a third Olympic gold in 1988 but had to be content with bronze.

breast-stroke), Bill Beaumont (and his bold leadership of England's Grand Slam-winning teams), Sandy Lyle (Scotland's Masters and Open-winning golfer), Daley Thompson (who dominated the decathlon), Nigel Mansell, Ayrton Senna and Alain Prost (whose high-speed rivalry brought Formula One on to the front pages), Mike Tyson (an emerging puncher of fearful power) and Sebastian Coe, Steve Cram and Steve Ovett (whose distance running lifted

Below: Steve Ovett (pictured), Seb Coe and Steve Cram dominated world middle-distance running throughout the 1980s.

Bottom: Adrian Moorhouse powers to victory in the 100 metres breast-stroke at the 1990 Commonwealth Games.

the sport to a new high). And then there were the men and women from the tennis circuit — Boris Becker, Ivan Lendl, John McEnroe, Stefan Edberg and Steffi Graf, who at 19 won her first Grand Slam, Martina Navratilova and Chris Evert. Oh yes, and a horse called Desert Orchid.

The decade began in earnest when Beaumont led England to the Grand Slam in rugby, but it was a brutal winter for the game with Welshman Paul Ringer sent off for a late and dangerous tackle on England outside half John Horton at Twickenham. He was the first player sent off at Twickenham in an international match since 1925, when John Brownlie of New Zealand was dismissed.

Above: Desert Orchid won the Cheltenham Gold Cup in 1989 as well as four victories in the King George VI.

Opposite: Bill Beaumont led England to Grand Slam success in 1980, their first since 1957.

COE, CRAM AND OVETT

Never has there been a more exciting period for English middle-distance running than the 1980s when Steve Ovett and Sebastian Coe set up a fierce rivalry and Steve Cram burst on to the scene to match them stride for stride. It was undoubtedly a golden age of British athletics. All three delivered world and Olympic titles in abundance, the like of which has never been repeated.

Between the late 1970s and mid-1980s, Ovett set two world records for the mile and one for the 1,500 metres. At the 1980 Moscow Olympics he won gold in the 800 and bronze in the 1,500.

Their intense rivalry was echoed by their conflicting personalities. Ovett refused to speak to the media following a post-race argument at Crystal Palace, while Coe, on the other hand, was eloquent and eminently approachable. Most of the press were rooting for the younger, smoother Coe, while the public went for the irascible rebel.

At Moscow the conventional wisdom was that Coe, as world record holder, would win the 800 metres and Ovett the 1,500. In the end the opposite happened and more than a decade after Moscow, Coe, who finished second in the shorter race, said: 'The 800 metres I ran had inexperience and nerves written all over it.' It was the one permanent blot on Coe's outstanding career which also won him another 1,500 gold at the 1984 Los Angeles Games and another 800 silver. In all Coe won nine outdoor world records, three of them set within 42 days in 1979.

While Coe and Ovett were enjoying their rivalry, Steve Cram was rapidly developing into the runner who would eclipse them both, finally stepping out of their shadow in 1983 when he won the 1,500 metres at the inaugural world championships in Helsinki. Second behind Coe at the 1984 Olympic 1,500 metre race, Cram had a momentous season the following year when he set three world records in 19 days. It established him as the third great British middle-distance runner of his generation.

Above: Alan Minter. In March 1980, Minter outboxed Vito Antuofermo at Caesar's Palace to win the world middleweight title.

The Moscow Olympics' opening ceremony saw seven of the 81 teams taking part, including Britain, performing some sort of boycott; the British chose to be represented at the opening jamboree by a single team member carrying the Olympic flag, a protest at the Russian invasion of Afghanistan. A total of 65 member countries refused to take part, most following a lead set by the United States.

Muhammad Ali, having retired officially, went on to fight, aged 38, with Larry Holmes and lose while in boxing's saddest story of the year — if not the decade — the British and European bantamweight champion Johnny Owen died in a Los Angeles hospital, seven weeks after being

SHERGAR STOLEN

It remains one of the great mysteries of modern sport. On February 9, 1983, a wonder horse named Shergar, who had been retired to the Aga Khan's Ballymany Stud in Co. Kildare, was taken from his stable by Irish Republican terrorists. It has always been believed, though never proved, that the horse was subsequently slaughtered after ransom demands were not met, partly because the horse was part of a syndicate. The criminals have never been brought to justice for a crime that shocked the racing world.

When he raced in the Derby of 1981, Shergar was a certainty, beginning the race, on soft ground, at 11-10 on. It was not so much a race as a procession as Walter Swinburn took his mount further and further away from the rest to win by ten lengths — the widest margin at the time in the history of the race. 'I was just a passenger on a very good horse,' Swinburn, who was only 19 at the time, later explained.

Above and left: Ian Botham batted and bowled England to victory in the 1981 Ashes in one of the greatest individual performances ever seen on a cricket field.

knocked out by Lupe Pintor of Mexico. Alan Minter, who won the world middleweight boxing championship in Las Vegas, defeating Vito Antuofermo, lost it six months later to Marvin Hagler at Wembley in a bout that ended after only three rounds, but which sparked dreadful hooliganism. In football, Brian Clough's Nottingham Forest beat Hamburg to win the European Cup for the second year in succession, having defeated Malmo of Sweden in Munich in 1979.

In 1981, England revelled in what later became known as 'Botham's Ashes'. At Headingley, in July, they were made to follow on against Australia, but fought back to claim an unlikely but inspiring win. Ian Botham hit 149 not out, Bob Willis took eight for 43 and England won by 18 runs. What a summer — it also saw McEnroe beat Bjorn Borg to secure his first Wimbledon title and Norway beat England at football. The same year saw the death of the wonderful motorcyclist Mike Hailwood, aged 40, in a car crash when he went out to buy some fish and chips.

As 'Mike the Bike', Hailwood won nine world titles and a record 14 Tourist Trophy races on the Isle of Man. In horse racing, Bob Champion and Aldaniti won an emotional victory at the Grand National, Champion triumphing less than two years after being told he had only eight months to live because of cancer. Another famous horse, Shergar, won the King George VI and Queen Elizabeth Diamond Stakes at Ascot, while in the winter cricket tour of the West Indies, in 1980-81, Ian Botham was named captain and the tour manager Ken Barrington, once a great England batsman, died after a heart attack.

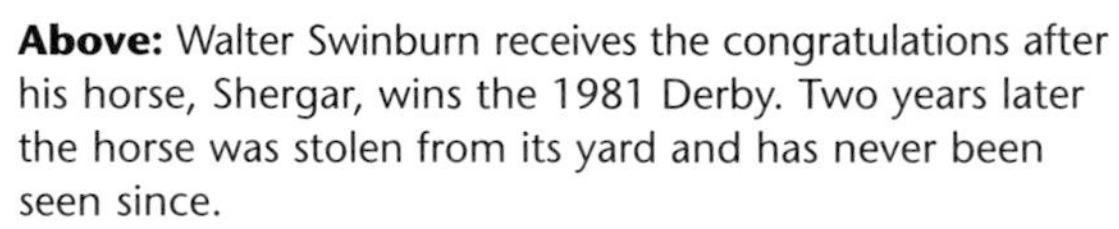

Above: Walter Swinburn receives the congratulations after his horse, Shergar, wins the 1981 Derby. Two years later the horse was stolen from its yard and has never been seen since.

Above right: John Francome – the champion jockey of the decade.

In the same year, Carl Lewis leapt 28 feet and seven and three-quarter inches, Nigel Mansell began his Formula One career with Lotus and a goal from left-back Alan Kennedy brought Liverpool a 1-0 win over Real Madrid in the Paris final of the European Cup. It was their third win in five years and, for Bob Paisley, the manager, it sealed a remarkable record. And, on a hot summer's night in Florence, Sebastian Coe broke the 800 metres world record, following it a month later with a mile record in Zurich.

In 1982, Bobby Robson succeeded Ron Greenwood as manager of England after the former West Ham manager had stepped down, following the 1982 World Cup finals in Spain. It was, for the first time, truly obvious that the job had become football's most poisoned chalice. Italy — led impressively by the goal-scoring ability of Paolo Rossi — won the competition, beating West Germany 3-1 in the final, but the lasting memory was of the French exit, after extra time, at the hands of the Germans on a rough and hot night in Seville where they lost 5-4 on penalties.

Other happenings saw the so-called 'dirty dozen' rebel cricketers, who took part in a tour of South Africa, return to England. They included Geoff Boycott and Alan Knott, both of whose Test careers were effectively ended by a three-year ban from the Test and County Cricket Board. In motor racing, Gilles Villeneuve was killed in a terrible accident in practice for the Belgian Grand Prix and in ice-

HILLSBOROUGH.
LIVERPOOL FANS CRUSHED.
96 DEAD.

Above: The 1984 Olympic 1500 metres final. Steve Cram (left) who won silver, congratulates Seb Coe on winning gold.

Top: Zola Budd (left) was blamed for tripping the race favourite, Mary Decker-Slaney (right) during the Olympic 3,000 metres final in Los Angeles.

skating, Torvill and Dean continued to entrance and succeed.

In 1983, India came to England to play in the cricket World Cup finals and won, defeating the favourites, the West Indies, who wasted a perfect opportunity of achieving their ambitions. At this time, a little-known Scottish football manager, Alex Ferguson, was starting to string together one of the most sensational career records in the

DAVIS SETS NEW STANDARDS

Steve Davis dominated the snooker scene throughout the 1980s when he lifted six world championship titles and stamped his irrefutable mark on the game.

A master tactician, Davis played with remarkable technical expertise and, after turning professional in 1978, gave an indication of what he would achieve when, on his world snooker championship debut in 1980 he defeated reigning champion Terry Griffiths in the second round. The Davis era began in earnest as he lifted the first of his world titles the following year, and although he was beaten by Tony Knowles in the defence of his title, he bounced back by becoming the 1983 and 1984 champion.

The ginger-haired maestro then lost the next two finals — beaten memorably 18-17 on the final black by Dennis Taylor in 1985 – but again, showing the resolve and determination which made him famous, Davis emphatically clinched the 1987, 1988 and 1989 titles.

Renowned for his exemplary safety game, which opened up opportunities that Davis rarely relinquished, he also claimed more than 15 other major titles during a glittering career, including the British Open championship, UK Open, and Benson and Hedges Masters.

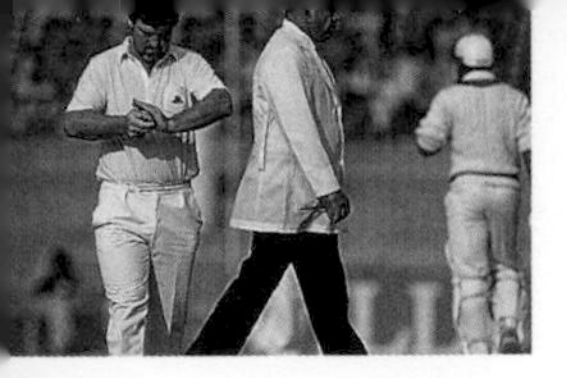

DISASTERS

Sadly, the 1980s will be remembered for three appalling football-related disasters as much as for all the good things that took place in sport. Heysel, Hillsborough and Bradford were all equally tragic and any one of them would have marred an otherwise prolific sporting decade. The fact that they all occurred within a few years of each other scarred the 1980s in a way few could ever have imagined.

First, tragically, there was Bradford when, on May 11, 1985, one deceptively innocent puff of smoke in the far corner of the main grandstand gave way to an inferno that engulfed an entire wooden structure. Within minutes, 41 people had lost their lives with a further 150 seriously injured. Images of panic-stricken and terror-struck fans were flashed around the world as bodies were dragged out of the fire.

If Bradford was an accident waiting to happen, as some believed, the same could not be said about the Heysel disaster just a fortnight later. Thirty-nine spectators, most of them supporters of Juventus, died when Liverpool fans ran riot before the European Cup final in Brussels. For some reason the game was allowed to proceed after police and ambulance men had cleared the terraces of the dead and injured. Juventus won 1-0 although no one really cared. English clubs were banned from European competition for five years and the effect was devastating. The ensuing loss of high-level competition ensured that English clubs were left behind in terms of technique and tactics.

Then, four years later, there was Hillsborough, the worst sporting disaster this century. A staggering 96 people lost their lives after being crushed to death at the Nottingham Forest-Liverpool FA Cup semi-final at Sheffield Wednesday's Hillsborough stadium. Shortly before kick-off there were still thousands of Liverpool fans milling outside the ground. To relieve congestion, a senior police officer made the fateful decision to open one of the huge metal gates at the Leppings Lane end of the ground. As the game began, the Liverpool supporters poured through.

Scores of fans were trampled underfoot or crushed against perimeter fencing. The game was halted after six minutes and the sheer magnitude of the disaster became apparent. Bodies were lifted forward, the dead covered with their own clothes. Anfield was turned into a shrine in the days that followed. Football stadiums were never the same again as fences were removed and all-seater grounds introduced.

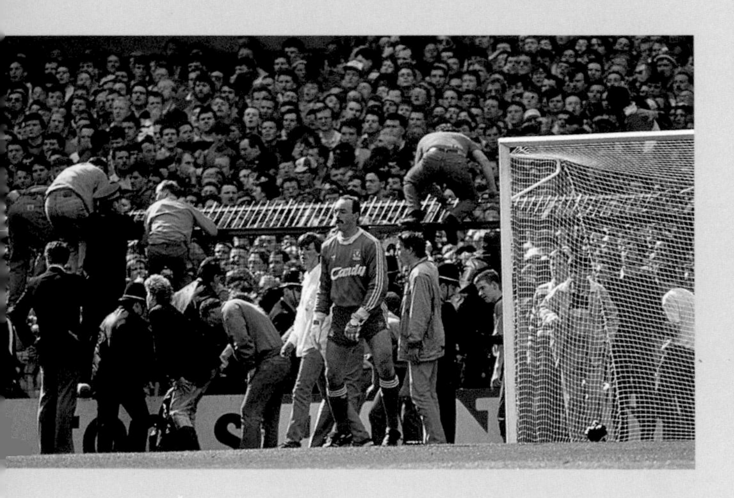

history of football by taking Aberdeen into Europe and winning the European Cup Winners' Cup. They defeated famous and majestic Real Madrid, the princes of European football, 2-1. In the first world championship of athletics, Carl Lewis won three gold medals, but his fellow-Americans lost yachting's America's Cup to Australia.

The following year, a little South African long-distance runner named Zola Budd became a British citizen shortly before her 18th birthday and thus avoided a nine-year qualification period; a Spaniard, Severiano Ballesteros enhanced his popularity with British crowds by winning the British Open golf title for a second time; and champion jockey John Francome retired, after a bad fall and 1,138 winners. In the European Football Championship, hosts France beat Spain 2-0 in the final, with Michel Platini the architect of their success and the finest goalscorer in the tournament with nine goals. In the Los Angeles Olympics, Daley Thompson strolled to gold, his second in succession in the games, in the decathlon. He was dubbed

'Superman' by some and described as the greatest all-round athlete of all time by experienced reporters. Carl Lewis won four gold medals.

In 1985, everything else was overshadowed by Bradford and Heysel. Bernard Hinault of France equalled the records set by Jacques Anquetil and Eddy Mercx by winning his fifth Tour de France; Barry McGuigan won the world featherweight boxing title, defeating Panama's Eusebio Pedroza; and Tony Jacklin captained the European Ryder Cup team to victory against the United States for the first time in 28 years. If that was not enough for the golfers, they also had another triumphant celebration to enjoy — with the sight of Sandy Lyle winning the British Open, the first Briton to do so since Jacklin himself in 1969.

At Wimbledon, a 17-year-old unseeded German called Boris Becker won the men's singles championship, the youngest player to do so. In football, Everton won the European Cup Winners' Cup, beating Rapid Vienna 3-1.

The next year, 1986, was the year of old and young and of cheats and heroes. The old came in the form of Jack Nicklaus who became the oldest winner of the US Masters, at the age of 46, and the young in the form of Mike Tyson, the youngest winner of the world heavyweight boxing championship in history, following his defeat of Trevor Berbick. The cheat was Diego Maradona, who leapt to punch the ball into England's net during Argentina's quarter-final victory at the Azteca Stadium in Mexico City. The goal became known as the 'Hand of God'.

Below: The Hand of God. Diego Maradona's hand-ball goal at the 1986 World Cup in Mexico cheated England out of a probable semi-final place.

TORVILL AND DEAN – THE ICE-SKATING PHENOMENON

It was the quintessential sporting partnership. It had skill, grace, flamboyancy, heaps of mystique and a piquancy that made your spine tingle. No one will ever forget how Jayne Torvill and Christopher Dean took ice dancing into a new and untapped sphere as they won four world titles and the 1984 Olympic gold medal, the latter with their haunting, breathtaking interpretation of Ravel's Bolero.

It was one of the most memorable and dramatic moments in the history of sport, not least for the fact that it sparked endless rumours about the relationship between the two off the ice. Such rumours were unfounded. In September, 1990, Torvill married Phil Christensen, while Christopher married the French-Canadian dancer Isabelle Duchesnay.

Torvill and Dean had joined forces as early as 1975 after dancing with separate partners. Their chemistry was instant as they won title after title, culminating in that remarkable, if controversial, Balero routine in Sarajevo which drew a maximum six points for artistic impression from each of the nine judges. Throughout their career, they received 136 marks of six and later turned professional, taking their ice show across the world.

Above: Mike Gatting and Shakoor Rana failed to see eye-to-eye during England's 1987 tour of Pakistan.

Argentina, inspired by the chunky-thighed little dynamo, went on to win the final against West Germany proving, perhaps, that sometimes the cheats can prosper. The hero, however, was Lloyd Honeyghan, who flew to Atlantic City where he was expected to be soundly beaten by Don Curry, but instead delivered one of boxing's great upsets by winning the world title. Honeyghan's surprise triumph was in contrast to the agony of Nigel Mansell who flew to Australia and lost out in his quest for the Formula One world championship because he suffered a tyre blow-out on his Williams car in the Australian Grand Prix in Adelaide. Alain Prost won the title by two points.

In 1987, Tyson became champion of all three heavyweight boxing titles, unifying them and proving himself beyond doubt to be the most

ENGLAND'S GRAND SLAM – 1980

Steve Smith, England's full-back has good reason to remember the 1980 Grand Slam because he nearly lost it for England. In the final match versus Wales with the clock ticking England led 6-4. Smith tried a clearance kick that Alan Phillips charged down and the Welsh galloped 50 metres to score a try in the corner to lead 8-6. Steve said: 'I felt gutted. We were going to lose the game and I was on my hands and knees in the corner, while the rest of the team were behind the posts for the conversion. The only man to walk the 30 yards to see me was our great captain, Bill Beaumont. He put his hands on my shoulders, stood me up and uttered the words I will never forget: "Smithy you stupid prat."'

'However, they missed the conversion and in the dying moments Dusty Hare kicked a penalty from out wide and we won 9-8.'

BARRY MCGUIGAN – THE CLONES CYCLONE

Barry McGuigan was more than just a boxer. Nicknamed the 'Clones cyclone' he was one of those rare sportsmen who was able to bridge the political and religious divide in a country — in this case Northern Ireland — that for generations had been scarred by rampant Catholic and Protestant extremism and bloodshed. When McGuigan won the world featherweight championship in the summer of 1985, both sides of the rival communities in Northern Ireland joined forces to celebrate. Thousands rejoiced in the streets of the province after McGuigan beat Eusebio Pedroza of Panama at Queen's Park Rangers' football ground in London. He defended the title on several occasions before being upset by Steve Cruz on a stiflingly hot night in Las Vegas and retired. He returned briefly, but never again regained the world championship.

Above: Gary Lineker celebrates scoring England's first goal in their 3-0 win over Poland in the 1986 World Cup. Lineker scored 48 goals in 80 appearances for England, one short of Bobby Charlton's record.

Left: In 1986, in one of the greatest boxing upsets of the century, Lloyd Honeyghan claimed Don Curry's world welterweight title in Atlantic City.

lethal boxer on earth. Europe travelled to America and won the Ryder Cup against the United States at Muirfield Village in Ohio and Nick Faldo recovered his swing, and his success, to win the British Open at Muirfield with 18 straight pars in the final round.

In athletics, Ed Moses, he of the legendary stride, bushy face and unbeatable running and jumping, lost a 400 metres hurdles event for the first time in 122 races. In football, Coventry beat Tottenham Hotspur 3-2 in the FA Cup final with an extra-time own goal from the Spurs captain Gary Mabbutt while, in cricket, Mike Gatting enjoyed the game's most famous public row when he argued vehemently with Pakistani umpire Shakoor Rana. Gatting, who had suffered a broken nose from a delivery by West Indies' Michael Holding in 1986, was forced to apologise after a furious row in Faisalabad where their stormy disagreement halted play for the day.

Gatting continued making headlines of the right and the wrong kind in 1988 when it was discovered that he had invited a barmaid to his hotel room on his 31st birthday. The revelation cost him the England captaincy. Sandy Lyle continued his golfing progress by travelling to the United States to become the first British player to win the US Masters, but another Briton, known

IAN BOTHAM – ENGLAND'S GREATEST CRICKETER

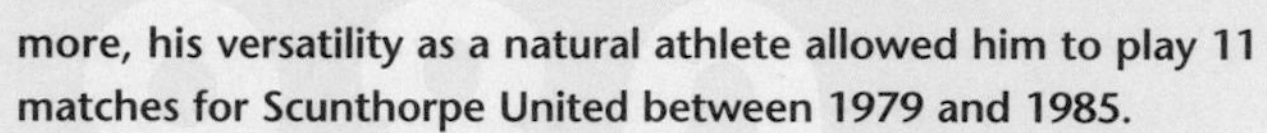

On an overcast day at Trent Bridge in July 1977, a star was born. A broad-shouldered youngster, just 21 years of age, stepped into the limelight of an Ashes series and obliterated the Australian batting order — a sensational debut befitting a man who would become one of England's cricketing greats. Botham possessed a complete range of batting strokes, each executed with supreme power and minimal effort, together with a varied array of bowling options. He was more than capable of swinging the ball in either direction, producing a tempting bouncer while mixing in a slower ball for good measure. Furthermore, his versatility as a natural athlete allowed him to play 11 matches for Scunthorpe United between 1979 and 1985.

More scintillating displays followed and in 1980 the English selectors, well aware of Botham's considerable influence on his fellow players, appointed him as captain for the two series' against West Indies. England lost them both, followed by the first Test of the 1981 Ashes series. The pressure forced him to relinquish the skipper's position, but he was quick to bounce back.

Under the leadership of Mike Brearley, England were forced to follow on in the third Test at Headingley. At 105 for 5, the home side were still 122 behind. Enter Beefy. With the bookmakers shouting impossible odds, the powerhouse smashed 149 not out to leave Australia needing 130 to win. Bob Willis did the rest with a brilliant 8-43 as England triumphed by 18 runs. The fourth Test followed at Edgbaston, with Australia set a tempting 151 for victory. Enter Botham the Bowler, scything through the Aussies once more. A 28-ball spell saw him grab five wickets for the loss of just one run as he notched up another match-winning performance.

Botham's cricketing prowess rewrote the record books. He compiled 383 wickets and 5200 runs for his country — a bowling average of 28.40 complimenting batting figures of 33.54 per Test — the best career figures of any all-rounder in the world.
In 1985 Botham undertook a long-distance charity walk from John o'Groats to Lands End. The sponsored feat was completed in less than six weeks and raised thousands of pounds for leukaemia research. More sponsored walks followed, including a 1988 trip across the Alps, and four years later, he was awarded the OBE for his services to the game and charity work.

as Eddie 'The Eagle' Edwards, achieved something more like lasting infamy when he entered the Olympic ski jumping contest and finished a distant last, making history, however, as the first Briton to compete in the event. Edwards' achievements were those of an enthusiastic amateur — a notion that was fading with time in the 1980s, as the 'transfer' of Welsh rugby union star Jonathan Davies, to a well-paid job in rugby league with Widnes proved. Money was everywhere now and no one was safe.

Left: Tessa Sanderson wins javelin gold at the Los Angeles Olympics in 1984.

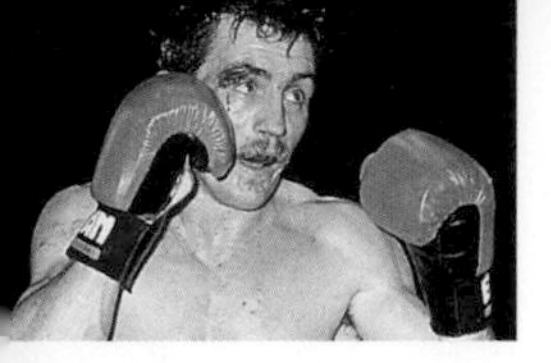

THE RYDER CUP REVIVAL YEARS

It was the moment a generation of golf fans had been waiting for. At 4.15pm on September 15, 1985, Sam Torrance holed a putt across the 18th green at The Belfry that echoed around the world. Torrance's birdie beat Andy North and gave Europe the Ryder Cup for the first time in 28 years. No sooner had his putt disappeared from sight than he was engulfed by ecstatic team members led by the captain, Tony Jacklin, who had won the Open championship back in 1969 and the US Open the following year. Concorde even rumbled overhead and dipped its wings in salute. It was the start of a thunderous European revival. Two years later, after a day of almost unbearable excitement, Europe retained the trophy, the first time they had done so — either as a full European team or as Great Britain & Ireland — on American soil. The competition continued to sway backwards and forwards across the Continent, each team narrowly beating the other. The Americans looked to have the cup back permanently when winning in 1991 and 1993 but by 1995 it was back in European hands and stayed that way two years later after an inspired piece of captaincy by the non-playing Seve Ballesteros in his native Spain.

In 1989, as the decade drew to a close, the rise of the new young sporting professional was a clear phenomenon. People were choosing sport as a career and working in it as a specialist, to maximise their incomes. No longer were sportsmen arriving as purists, people in search of a few pounds to help them pursue their fun. Agents and managers, too, were increasingly part of the scene and drugs, performance-enhancing and other, became more and more apparent. And these younger stars were confident of their own futures.

Stephen Hendry, only 20, showed he knew exactly what he was doing when he won the Benson and Hedges Masters snooker title. And 17-year-old American Michael Chang won the French Open tennis title, in the process becoming the youngest winner of a Grand Slam event. In golf, Nick Faldo won the first of his three Masters tournaments. But it was all marred, darkened and eclipsed by Hillsborough

Above: Dennis Taylor shocked Steve Davis and the snooker world when he beat the Englishman in the final of the 1985 world snooker championship.

Above: Eddie 'The Eagle' Edwards at the 1988 Winter Olympics, in Calgary. He finished last, by a distance, but received far more publicity than the competition winner.

Left: Kenny Dalglish lifts the 1986 FA Cup. It was just one of a cluster of trophies that went to Anfield during a decade of total domination.

KICKED WHERE IT HURTS

Nigel Mansell, former world drivers' champion first won the world title for the only time in 1992. He challenged the supremacy of Ayrton Senna and Alain Prost and when he left for American Indycars in 1993, did the same again over there. A proud family man, who sacrificed everything to achieve success early in his life, he threw himself wholeheartedly into everything. On one occasion this attitude resulted in an injury caused while playing in a media football match before the Spanish Grand Prix at Barcelona. The next day he limped around the paddock in pain, but still qualified brilliantly. Then, on Sunday morning, in the drivers' briefing, his friend Gerhard Berger decided on a bit of fun — and kicked Mansell's ankle. They ended up in a fight. 'I just wanted to see which ankle it was!' said Berger. Mansell was livid.

and the afternoon which reshaped English football, ushering in the Taylor Report and the era of new stadiums and new investment which has carried the game, on a wave of wealth and success, into the new millennium.

Liverpool went on to Wembley and won the FA Cup, beating city rivals Everton in an extraordinary and enthralling final, before entertaining Arsenal at home in their final league match six days later. Unbeaten in 24 games, they were favourites to win, but Arsenal had to win by two clear goals to take the championship on goals scored — and did so with Michael Thomas scoring two minutes into injury time, adding to an earlier goal from Alan Smith. The FA Cup final was a Liverpudlian community event of momentous feeling for the city, but their second double was to elude the team of the decade. It was an extraordinary finish to an unforgettable season and a momentous decade of British sport.

1990-1999

BIG BUSINESS

10

CHAMPIONS

YOUNGER AND YOUNGER, faster and faster, higher and higher, more and more.

The 1990s saw sport explode through the modern electronic media and become a rapidly-developing boom business, something now changed out of all recognition from the athletic past-times that once kept people busy at weekends. By the end of the decade and the end of the millennium, sport was a news-machine and money-machine that could dwarf many other industries. Stars rose and fell with alarming speed, their reputations fading as fast as they were made. Sponsorship marched in and took control with television acting as a more than willing accomplice to the corporate takeover.

Old characters of the century, the decade and the fading imagination died, others simply gave up the ghost and tragedy, as ever, lurked on every corner. The death of Ayrton Senna at Imola, 24 hours after Roland Ratzenberger had perished, showed that Formula One, for all its hype, smooth operators and a safety crusade initiated by Jackie Stewart and continued by Professor Sid Watkins, remained, like sport, a fatal attraction.

Yet it was a wonderful decade too. Full of fire and brimstone, colour, theatre and achievement. And the greatest success of all came at the end, in May 1999, when Manchester United flew to Barcelona and, two nights later flew home with the European Cup. By then, Europe's paramount football tournament had been re-named as the European Champions League and the runners-up in the domestic leagues around the continent were permitted to enter the competition. Manchester United, ironically, had qualified by just such a route, having finished behind Arsenal in the Premiership (the new name for

STEPHEN HENDRY

When Stephen Hendry claimed victory in the 1999 world snooker championships it was not only his seventh title, but it lifted him on to a plane which recognised him as the most successful player of the modern era, eclipsing six-time champions Ray Reardon and Steve Davis.

Showing the true characteristics of a champion by re-discovering the kind of form which saw him sweep all before him during his prime, Hendry attained the not-so elusive seventh victory which he knew would elevate him onto the highest mantle of individual success in the game. Hendry became the youngest-ever winner of the world championship at 21 years and 106 days and he went on to claim all the sport's major title.

An all-round talent, Hendry was especially recognised for his fluent break-building, long-potting prowess and ability to perform under the most intense of pressure. The latter was emphatically proven by a 147 break in the deciding frame of a final against Ronnie O'Sullivan, which Hendry won 10-9.

the old First Division in the age of new money and new media) the previous season.

United's win in Spain, with two goals in the final nail-biting minutes just as Bayern Munich were deciding on their victory speeches with a single goal lead, was as dramatic and stirring a night as sport could ever deliver. It completed a wonderful season for them, in which they had not only taken the giant European trophy home again for the first time in 31 years, but also the Premiership and FA Cup and so delivered the first such treble triumph in the history of English soccer.

United's heroes will be long remembered. Alex Ferguson, David Beckham, Peter Schmeichel, Ryan Giggs, Teddy Sheringham and Gary Neville are only a few of the braves who succeeded under enormous pressure. But they were only some of the men of a decade decorated with greatness and youth in sport. Showmanship, knowing where the cameras were positioned and how to 'ham' it up for a glamorous impression, was a quality of the age and expertly delivered by the stars.

From Stephen Hendry, aged 21 in 1990 when he became the youngest snooker world champion, to Michael Owen, who burst on to the world football scene in 1998, they were all men and women who knew what they were doing. The instinct, the flair and the natural ability — all of these were trained into a new shape and moulded into something that was intended to produce consistency and regularity. Success, bankable success, was the new aim. Glory was a secondary consideration.

So what happened? Well, 1990 saw the biggest upset in boxing history. James 'Buster' Douglas, a relatively unknown American boxer achieved the near impossible in Tokyo when he beat Mike Tyson with a 10th round knockout and took the world heavyweight championship, Richard Hadlee became a cricketing knight after retiring from the game having taken a record 400 Test wickets and, in a less-honourable moment, Alex Higgins, the snooker player, threatened to have Dennis Taylor, a rival player, shot.

Below: Chris Waddle is consoled by Germany's Lothar Matthaeus, after his penalty miss in the 1990 World Cup handed Germany a place in the final.

Bottom: The exploits of Greg Rusedski (pictured) and Tim Henman have raised the profile of British tennis to a level not seen since the great Fred Perry.

Above: The achievements of Graham Gooch, which included a knock of 333 against India in 1990, elevated him to the status of one of the all-time great batsmen.

In athletics, Steve Backley threw a javelin world record while, in football, Lord Justice Taylor's report, following his inquiry into the Hillsborough disaster of 1989, recommended that all-seater stadiums be introduced into the English First and Second Divisions by 1994.

Later in the summer, Italy hosted the World Cup finals in which Bobby Robson's England reached the last four, but lost on penalties to West Germany. Paul Gascoigne, who played well, wept. Nick Faldo won the US Masters and thereby became only the second man to make a successful defence of his title, while, in cricket, Graham Gooch hit 333 runs against India to join the ranks of the all-time great batsmen.

In 1991, the same Gascoigne, a mixture of clown and genius struck a wonderful free-kick goal for Tottenham at Wembley against Arsenal to win an FA Cup semi-final. In the final, against Nottingham Forest, however, he made a wild tackle and injured himself badly, ruining his career in the process. A transfer to Lazio, of Rome, beckoned and, though it went through later, his play was never quite the same again. In February, unexpectedly, Kenny Dalglish, who had shown such dignity and feeling through Liverpool's troubles in the late 1980s at Heysel and Hillsborough, resigned as manager, citing stress. 'The worst decision I could have made was not to make a decision,' he said. For Liverpool, it was the end of an era.

In rugby, England won the Five Nations and the Grand Slam, before suffering the disappointment of defeat in the World Cup final, going down 12-6 to their old foes Australia. In the track and field world championships in Tokyo, Liz McColgan, Scotland's Commonwealth champion, destroyed a top-class field in the 10,000 metres to win the gold medal with an awesome display of front-running. 'I have had very little money in my trust fund over the last year,' McColgan admitted after the race, highlighting the difference in financial backing between Britain's most popular sports and those vying to move into the 'elite'. In boxing, the world was saddened when Michael Watson fell into a coma following a 12th round defeat by Chris Eubank in a WBO super-middleweight clash in September.

In 1992, another athlete stole the show at the Olympic Games in Barcelona. Linford Christie, eyes bulging, a portrait of controlled aggression, used 'tunnel vision' to storm to 100 metres gold in the Montjuic Stadium in 9.96 seconds. The world's fastest human being immortalised himself as Britain's most successful athlete by defeating Americans Leroy Burrell and Dennis Mitchell, who had both dismissed his chances prior to the race.

In rugby, England, under Will Carling, repeated their Grand Slam success, while Eric Cantona inspired Leeds United and guided them to triumph in the English league championship, Gary Lineker was substituted by England manager Graham Taylor and missed out on a chance to beat Bobby Charlton's record of 49 international goals and Nigel Mansell, after a blistering start to the year with Williams, won the world drivers' championship in magnificent style. A contract dispute with the team, however, prevented him from defending the title the following year and he moved to the United States where he won the IndyCar championship in another rollercoaster season.

In horse racing, Rodrigo de Triano gave Lester Piggott his 30th British Classic winner as the 56-year-old rode to victory in the 2,000 Guineas at Newmarket, while in boxing, a points defeat of Jess Benavides gave Duke McKenzie the WBO super-bantamweight crown. More significantly, McKenzie became the first British fighter to claim world titles at

CHRIS EUBANK — THE MOST HATED MAN IN BOXING?

For every 100 heroes in sport, there is always room for a villain. A figure that most of the public love to hate, who, despite such loathing, uses his or her talent to reach the pinnacle of their chosen sport. In British boxing from the late 1980s, Chris Eubank adequately filled that void. The strutting, monocle-clad fighter, with a fondness for juggernauts and Harley-Davidson motorcycles, was always at odds with the fight-fans and his peers, but he was a promoter's dream. Many people bought tickets in the hope of seeing him beaten!

After gaining a reputation as a fearsome puncher with a lion heart after early fights in the United States, where he had relocated as a child, he returned to England. After an eighth-round stoppage of durable Agentine, Hugo Corti, in March 1990, he set his sights on Nigel Benn's WBO middleweight championship. The two unbeaten fighters clashed in November of the same year in Birmingham. Both fighters exuded pure hatred for each other. Benn, a popular explosive puncher from Ilford, fiercely proud of the fight-game, against Eubank, a snarling lion who openly despised what he described as 'a barbaric, filthy, disgusting' sport.

Round after round, both fighters pulverised each other until finally one of them broke. After taking severe body punishment, the underdog Eubank triumphed in a thrilling contest as the referee was forced to rescue a punched-out Benn in round nine. The eccentric Eubank was world champion.

Other fights followed before an infamous two-fight battle with fellow Briton Michael Watson, the second of which proved to have tragic consequences as Watson fell into a coma after a brutal fight.

After several low-key defences, the fight which the public wanted to see, 'Eubank-Benn II', went ahead in front of 42,000 avid fans at Old Trafford, Manchester. Both fighters stood toe-to-toe in an absorbing 12-round contest, which ended, controversially, in a draw. Eubank's unbeaten run, much to the delight of the watching public, came to an end in his 44th bout, his 15th WBO title defence, as Irishman Steve Collins beat him on points in Cork in March 1995, a feat he repeated six months later.

three different weights, having won the IBF flyweight title in 1988 and the WBO bantamweight championship in 1991. However, on a world level, fallen giant Mike Tyson was convicted of raping an 18-year-old beauty queen.

In golf, Nick Faldo continued to weave his magic as he won the British Open title again, the third time, the first man to do the treble in the championship since Henry Cotton in 1948.

By now sport was feeling heavy-laden with events and personalities. Television, itself expanding with channels, beamed more sport than ever before to more viewers than previously. Cynics carped, but it went on and on. So, in 1993, when two British boxers faced each other for the first time this century in a world heavyweight championship fight, it was a television event. Lennox Lewis beat Frank Bruno. In another televised sporting moment, Brian Clough retired from management after his Nottingham Forest team were relegated from the Premiership.

But by now other stars were rising fast. Colin Jackson and Sally Gunnell broke records in the world athletics championships in Stuttgart where Linford Christie added the 100 metres world gold to his Olympic title a year earlier.

FRANK BRUNO – CHAMPION AT THE FOURTH ATTEMPT

In the history of sport there have been few British sportsmen who have enjoyed such popularity as the big heavyweight, Frank Bruno. His loveable hero image, and 'Where's 'Arry' catch-phrase endeared him to millions, but until 1995 his boxing career had been hampered by failure.

When he won the WBC title from Oliver McCall in 1995 (it was his fourth attempt to claim a version of the world title) it was the end of an unbelievable odyssey for a man blessed with a fearsome punch, but cursed by a distinct lack of fighting instincts. His weak chin and tendency to crumble under pressure had seen him soundly beaten by Tim Witherspoon, Mike Tyson, and Lennox Lewis in his previous title challenges, but against McCall he showed immense heart to cling on for a deserved points victory. He lost the belt in his first defence to a resurgent Tyson, and then retired. But no one could deny that, for a brief period at least, he was champion of the world.

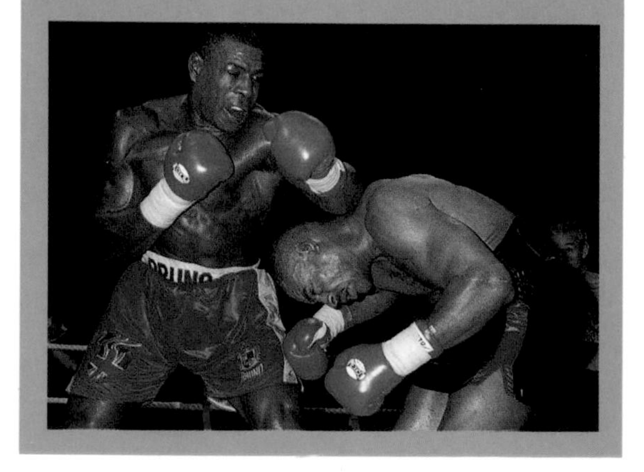

Above: Teddy Sheringham can barely contain his delight after his last-gasp equaliser against Bayern Munich in the 1999 Champions League final. His Manchester United side went on to win the trophy with almost the last kick of the game.

Right: Sally Gunnell's career achievements included a gold medal in the 400 metres hurdles at the Barcelona Olympics in 1992.

And what else? The Grand National was turned into a farce by a muddle with red flags and false starts following a delay caused by animal rights protesters, Monica Seles was stabbed, on court, by a spectator in Hamburg, and Nigel Mansell recovered from a huge accident on the Phoenix Oval; two British middleweight boxers, Chris Eubank and Nigel Benn slugged out a draw in Manchester in a bloody match, and Terry Venables battled with chairman Alan Sugar for control of Tottenham Hotspur after being dismissed.

In cycling, Chris Boardman, the reigning Olympic champion, shattered the world hour record as he powered to a distance of 52.27 kilometres before announcing his intention to turn professional and compete in the sport's blue riband event, the Tour de France. In rugby, the British Lions, captained by Scotland's Gavin Hastings, were narrowly defeated by New Zealand by two Tests to one despite leading 10-0 in the deciding match, and in cricket, Graeme Hick became the youngest batsman to score more than 20,000 runs in first-class cricket at the age of 27 years and 20 days, beating the record set by Wally Hammond in 1931.

The next year, 1994, Manchester United began to up the beat on their march to glory. They won the double, beating Chelsea 4-0 in the FA Cup final and, in the United States in the World Cup — for which England failed to qualify — Brazil beat Italy on penalties. In cricket, Brian Lara scored 375 for the West Indies against England, while in horse racing, Willie Carson, aged 51, won the Derby, riding a horse called Erhaab.

Jimmy White, one of the nation's best loved sportsman, suffered his fifth successive world snooker final defeat, his sixth in all, as Stephen Hendry triumphed 18-17 to beat his rival for the

GASCOIGNE'S TEARS

This is one of the most endearing sports pictures of the decade. A tearful Paul Gascoigne salutes the English fans after England's heart-breaking semi-final defeat at the hands of Germany in the 1990 World Cup. Sadly for Gascoigne, there were to be more tears in the years that followed.

During his career for Newcastle and Tottenham Hotspur, 'Gazza' was adored by millions and was undoubtedly the greatest talent to grace a football field since George Best, but, like his predecessor, Gascoigne's genius was similarly flawed. He was noted for his volatile temperament, a temperament that reached boiling point, playing for Spurs against Nottingham Forest in the FA Cup final of 1991. He had scored a goal in almost every round during Spurs' 1991 cup run, and those he hadn't scored he had created. Following another blistering display against North London arch-rivals, Arsenal, in the semi-final, the stage was set. But his ludicrous challenge on Forest's Gary Charles in the opening minutes of the match caused him to suffer serious knee ligament damage.

He recovered to continue his career with Italian club Lazio, Rangers, and Middlesbrough, but in truth he has never played as well since. There was further heartbreak when he was controversially omitted from Glenn Hoddle's 1998 World Cup squad, the manager unimpressed by the wayward star's clowning antics and late night high jinks in the run-up to the tournament. Gazza's tears and subsequent rage were indicative of the realisation that his last chance to impose himself on a world stage had undoubtedly gone.

third final in a row, but on a happier note, Devon Malcolm, playing at The Oval in the third Test against South Africa, achieved the sixth best bowling figures in cricket history. His nine for 57 helped England to an eight-wicket win.

In 1995, as the pace grew ever more hectic, in life as in sport, so the events blurred together. This year saw the Cantona controversy when Eric, playing for Manchester United, jumped into the crowd at Crystal Palace and kicked a fan, and Blackburn, with a team built with the funds supplied by their rich chairman Jack Walker, won the English Premier League; in cricket, Dominic Cork took a hat-trick as England beat the West Indies at Old Trafford. Jonathan Edwards leapt to a triple-jump world record, and the Football Association launched an inquiry into the dealings of George Graham, the Arsenal manager, which led to his eventual sacking.

Frank Bruno, in his fourth attempt at a world heavyweight boxing crown, finally succeeded with a points victory over Oliver McCall, the man who had earlier defeated Lennox Lewis for the WBC crown. Sheffield-born Prince Naseem Hamed achieved his lifelong dream of winning a world title with an eighth round stoppage of Welshman Steve Robinson in a WBO world featherweight contest. Tim Henman, partnering Jeremy Bates, was disqualified from the Wimbledon men's doubles competition after striking ball-girl, Caroline Hall. The pair made up quickly in front of the national press. And 12 years after her first success with Corbiere,

Opposite top: Will Carling led England to Grand Slams in 1991 and 1992 during a golden age for English rugby.

Top right: Steve Backley became the first British athlete to break the javelin world record. He has won two Commonwealth titles and the European Championships three times, but never an Olympic gold.

Right: Willie Carson, aged 51, capped a glittering flat career by winning the 1994 Derby, riding Erhaab.

GOODYEAR
B&H
MasterCard
HONDA

trainer Jenny Pitman returned to the Grand National winners' enclosure when Royal Athlete, a 40-1 long-shot, crossed the line to win the historic Aintree race.

The next year, 1996, saw football come home. England hosted the finals of the European Championship, reached the semi-finals and followed the modern tradition by losing to Germany on penalties. England's manager Terry Venables later decided to step down from the job after a long spell of hostile reports about his business activities outside football. Glenn Hoddle took over, but he lasted only until early 1999. In the 1998 World Cup finals in France, the previous summer, a defeat by Argentina in

Opposite: Damon Hill celebrates victory in the Belgian Grand Prix in August 1998, driving for Jordan. In 1996, while with Williams, he won the world drivers' championship he so craved.

A JOKE SHARED WITH THOUSANDS

Brian Johnston was a legendary cricket commentator, whose astute observations and moments of humour lit up many a Test match. One of the many anecdotes that helped endear 'Jonners', as he was known, to so many people, concerned an hilarious piece of commentary involving Ian Botham in the final Test against the West Indies in 1991.

When fellow BBC radio commentator Jonathan Agnew, with a deliberately mischievous double entendre, referred to Botham's attempt to hurdle the bails as 'trying to get his leg over,' Johnston was lost for words as he fell about laughing in the studio. 'Oh do stop it, Aggers' became one of the legendary quotes of radio commentary as Jonners tried desperately to regain his composure. There followed a lengthy period of near-silence on air, punctuated only by Brian almost choking with laughter.

MANSELL MASTERY

The 'charger' of Grand Prix racing during the 1980s and early 1990s, Nigel Mansell won his place in the heart of British sport with his exploits in Formula One which culminated in him winning the 1992 world drivers' championship.

Mansell claimed nine wins and 14 pole positions in the 16 races that year for Williams when he accumulated a points tally of 108 — almost double the 56 of his team-mate Riccardo Patrese.

Mansell's win was a popular and long-awaited one for British fans who had seen the Midlands-born driver finish runner-up on three previous occasions. The most agonising of these was in 1986 when he was just two points off eventual champion Alain Prost.

Noted for his racing pedigree, Mansell duelled with Ayrton Senna and Prost regularly during his career, and as a result, Grand Prix racing enjoyed a huge popularity boom. One of the most famous racing battles took place when Mansell was wheel-to-wheel with Senna as the sparks flew in the Spanish Grand Prix in 1992.

Beginning his Grand Prix career with Lotus in 1980, he also had spells at Williams and Ferrari and savoured his first Formula One win on home territory when he clinched the European Grand Prix at Brands Hatch in 1985. In 1992, after clinching the drivers' championship, Mansell chose the moment to bow out of Formula One and cross the Atlantic to compete on the American Indycar circuit. The consummate professional, he made the transition with ease, winning the championship in his first year.

Above: Linford Christie became Britain's greatest ever 100 metres sprinter when, in Barcelona in 1992, he added the Olympic gold medal to his other many other achievements.

Right: English hearts sink as David Beckham is sent off in the 1998 World Cup. The pictures of his dismissal, against Argentina, were beamed around the world.

GET PROTECTION

Women's cricket has never quite taken off but if there is one female player of whom every fan has heard, it is England's former captain, Rachel Heyhoe Flint. Rachel was a ceaseless campaigner for women to be admitted into one of the last male bastions in sport — the Pavilion at Lord's — finally achieving her goal in 1998. Once, at a dinner party, a persistent male diner wished to find out if women cricketers wore a protective box and chest pads. Rachel replied: 'We certainly do, but we use a pair of coconuts and a man-hole cover.'

St Etienne provided both some of the most illustrious football of the tournament and some of the most petulant behaviour. David Beckham was sent off and Argentina beat England's 10-man team on penalties.

Back to 1996 and Frankie Dettori rode seven winners in one day at Ascot, at odds of more than 25,000-1; Frank Bruno retired; and Aston Villa won the Football League Cup for a record fifth time. Alan Shearer became the world's most expensive player (one of many now on a wild spiral of lavish overspending in the sport) when he moved from Blackburn to Newcastle for £15 million; and Damon Hill, the man who filled the breach at Williams as team leader following Ayrton Senna's death at Imola in 1994, won the world drivers' championship by cruising to victory in the Japanese Grand Prix at Suzuka. Steve Redgrave sobbed with joy as he became Britain's greatest ever Olympian by winning a fourth successive gold medal in rowing as he retained his coxless pairs title with Matthew Pinsent.

And what else since, in the last three years? What quick memories to be revived now? A few names to help: Ronnie O'Sullivan, Tim Henman, Michael Owen, Phil Tufnell's sensational 11-93 to bowl out the Australian's at The Oval in 1997. Also in 1997, the Grand National was again disrupted, this time by a bomb threat, forcing the race to be postponed until the following Monday. Lord Gyllene won

the rescheduled event in front of a crowd of more than 20,000. Greg Rusedski, after reaching the quarter-finals at Wimbledon, moved into the final of the US Open before losing to Australian Patrick Rafter in four sets and in golf, Spanish legend Seve Ballesteros skippered Europe to victory over America in the Ryder Cup at Valderrama.

In 1998, Arsenal rose to the challenge of Manchester United by pulling off another double, only the second club to do it twice, 27 years after their first success in 1971; and legendary cricket umpire Dickie Bird announced his retirement from the game. In athletics, Darren Campbell emulated his coach, Linford Christie, and landed the European 100 metres title ahead of compatriot Dwain Chambers, while Denise Lewis emerged as the top women's track and field star with gold in the heptathlon.

Kevin Keegan, such a fine player with Liverpool in their pomp, took over from Hoddle as England manager after a dramatic run with

Above: England captain, Alan Shearer, became the domestic game's most expensive player when he signed for Newcastle from Blackburn Rovers for a record £15 million, in 1996.

NICK FALDO – THE GOLFING ICE-MAN

No one can under-estimate the influence that Nick Faldo has had on British and European golf over a decade, embracing both the 1980s and 1990s. He won the US Masters in 1989 and the following year carved a special place in sporting history when he became only the second man to successfully defend the title, beating Ray Floyd in a play-off after coming from four behind with six to play to tie the American. He won again in 1996, beating the unfortunate Greg Norman, after the Australian had led by six strokes going into the final round.

Faldo won the Open championship in 1987 and 1990, and then, in 1992 he won the Claret Jug for the third time, the first person to do so since Henry Cotton in 1948. Despite his reputation as an inward-looking loner who had a deep distrust of the media and didn't always get on with his peers, Faldo's inspiration and experience played a major role in helping the European Ryder Cup team gain parity with, and ultimately beat, the previously dominant Americans.

Above: Michael Atherton came under scrutiny in the summer of 1994 for alleged ball-tampering during the Test against South Africa.

Top: In 1999 Kevin Keegan, the former captain of his country, made the transition to England manager. His team beat Poland 3-1 on March 27, in his first game in charge.

Left: A proven Test batsman, Alec Stewart could not cope with the triple responsibility of batsman, wicket-keeper and captain as England lurched from one loss to another in the late 1990s. He was replaced as captain, in June 1999, by Nasser Hussain.

SIR ALEX FERGUSON'S TREBLE

Daring, vibrant and superstar-laden, Manchester United dominated English football in the 1990s before stamping their mark on the European scene when they tasted success in one of the most dramatic wins in European, if not world, football. Recovering from an early goal deficit United, a team famous for their stamina, scored two late goals to break the hearts of their German rivals, Bayern Munich, in the Nou Camp, Barcelona and secure their third major trophy of the season. They had earlier won the domestic league and cup double.

David Beckham, Ryan Giggs, Eric Cantona, and Peter Schmeichel — a gigantic presence in goal and a stalwart of their success who left Old Trafford at the end of the 1999 season — were just some of the illustrious names who played a pivotal role in their decade of brilliance. But on a May night in Barcelona the glory rested with two late substitutes, Teddy Sheringham and Ole Gunnar Solskjaer, who scored the vital goals. In fact both players had played merely bit-parts over the entire season, but their dynamic impact, just when it was most needed, illustrated more than anything the talented squad and strength in depth which Ferguson had assembled.

Ferguson took charge of an under-achieving team in November 1986 but took some time to turn the club's fortunes around. But their success in the 1990s, which included five league titles, four FA Cup wins, European Cup Winners' Cup and that famous treble victory — eclipsing the achievements of their great rivals, Liverpool who dominated the 1980s — may never be surpassed.

Newcastle, and then Fulham, as the Football Association scrambled around for straws to grasp in the windy winter of 1998-1999.

It was impossible to move at the end of the century without Manchester United appearing somewhere amid the plethora of sport that jammed the news, business and features pages of newspapers every day. Football was booming and it was a measure of its popularity that the protracted transfer wrangle involving Nicolas Anelka to Real Madrid stayed among the top news stories throughout the summer.

In athletics, it was bad news for another great institutional figurehead as Linford Christie failed a routine drugs test. His reputation was smeared, but he shouted his innocence before the focus of attention moved to Seville and the world championships.

Such disappointments were par for the course in tennis, too, as Tim Henman succumbed again to Pete Sampras at Wimbledon — the American going on to defeat compatriot Andre Agassi in the final — but not in golf. Paul Lawrie, hailing from Scotland, won the British Open on home soil to the delight of a throng of patriots on the final day at Carnoustie. But it was in the arena of cricket, in which England had started the century with

A NEW BREED OF FOOTBALLING LEGEND

Just when English football was crying out for new stars to boost its presence on the world stage and capture the imagination of its fans, Michael Owen and David Beckham rose to the challenge in emphatic and breath-taking style at the 1998 World Cup, in France.

Beckham, who proved on the world stage his passing accuracy and threatening ability to open up opposition defences, produced a free-kick of power and accuracy to stun Colombia. Owen showed no indication of his youth when, 18 at the time, he scored a wonderful goal against Argentina in the second round which left onlookers gasping.

Hailing from London, Beckham fulfilled a dream when he was signed up as a youngster by Manchester United, while Owen, the youngest-ever England international to be capped when he made his debut against Chile at Wembley aged 18 years and 59 days, came through the famous Anfield ranks of Liverpool to create his own story.

Above: Chris Boardman broke the world hour record in September 1996 with a distance of 52.27 kilometres. He was already the world individual pursuit champion and the world 4000 metres record holder.

Right: Martin Offiah was the record try scorer in his first four seasons in rugby league. In 1992 he signed for Wigan, who dominated the sport throughout the 1980s and 1990s.

such strong hopes and so many big names, that they faded at the end. A string of captains did little to revive the team in the summer when Australia came and took the World Cup home and New Zealand proved to be stubborn and often embarrassing opponents. A self-inflicted trial began. It was typical of British sport and its character, but it demonstrated its importance as a golden era came to a conclusion at the end of a truly great British sporting century.

Above: Steve Redgrave (right) and Matthew Pinsent celebrate victory in the coxless pairs at the 1996 Olympic Games. It was Redgrave's fourth consecutive Olympic gold medal in the event.

THE REVIVAL OF BRITISH TENNIS

It seemed British tennis had been permanently in the doldrums as the 20th century drew to a close, but with the sport crying out for heroes to cheer, Tim Henman and Greg Rusedski duly arrived to fill the huge void.

The pair thrust themselves on the international scene, almost in unison during the mid-1990s, and gave British fans the icons they had craved for so long. They gave promise of winning on home territory at Wimbledon as well as the sport's other major tournaments.

Rusedski, who switched nationality from Canadian in 1995, was the first to make his mark as he became the first Briton to reach a Grand Slam final in 59 years when he lost in the US Open in 1997. Losing to Pat Rafter, Rusedski could take solace in the fact that his performance was enough to make him the first Briton ever to enter the top 10 in the world rankings as he climbed to number four soon afterwards.

Not to be outdone, Henmania swept Wimbledon as Henman showed that he, along with Rusedski, had the promise to give the country its first home victory since Fred Perry claimed the last of his three successive titles in 1936. Born in Oxford in 1974, Henman reached the quarter-finals in 1996 and 1997 before improving to reach the semi-finals in 1998 and 1999. But in each of his last four outings he was beaten by eventual, and record six-time Wimbledon winner, Pete Sampras.

Henman himself broke into the top 10 in 1998 as Rusedski dropped out, but both were firm challengers on the world circuit. Henman, a classy performer with natural serve-volleying prowess, and Rusedski, the most powerful server in the men's game, both had the games capable of realising Grand Slam success.

INDEX

INDEX

PICTURE CREDITS

All pictures are provided courtesy of Popperfoto unless stated

Allsport 98 (top), 102-103, 108

Graham Gooch 142

Hulton Getty 11, 13, 18, 44 (top), 67 (bottom), 73 (top), 74, 98 (bottom)

Popperfoto/Reuters 138-139, 140, 141 (bottom), 143-145, 146 (top), 147 (top), 148, 150-155

Tom Finney 61 (top)

Chapter Opener photographs are as follows:

Chapter One WG Grace (1848-1914) shown bowling.

Chapter Two CB Fry. His achievements, most notably in cricket and football, transcended sport.

Chapter Three Thousands of fans spill on to the pitch before the start of the 1923 FA Cup final.

Chapter Four The Bodyline Series. Australian batsman Bill Woodfull drops his bat after being hit with a ball from England's Harold Larwood.

Chapter Five John Mark of Cambridge University lights the Olympic Flame, at Wembley Stadium in 1948.

Chapter Six Roger Bannister breaks the four-minute mile barrier, Oxford, May 6, 1954.

Chapter Seven Bobby Moore kisses the Jules Rimet trophy after England's World Cup triumph over West Germany.

Chapter Eight JPR Williams battles through the South African line during the British Lions' tour of 1974.

Chapter Nine Seb Coe wins gold in the 1500 metres at the 1984 Los Angeles Olympics.

Chapter Ten Alex Ferguson and his Treble-winning team lift the European Cup, Barcelona, May 1999.